The Rich Woods of Union County

A Comprehensive History of Richwood, Ohio

Charles Barry
Dustin K. Lowe

Lake Baccarat Press
Richwood, Ohio

Published by Lake Baccarat Press
An imprint of Dustin Lowe Publishing

Library of Congress Control Number: 2021904366

Images obtained with permission by Charles Barry and the Richwood-North Union Public Library

Manufactured in the United States of America

ISBN: 978-0-578-85292-8 (paperback)
ISBN: 978-0-578-88702-9 (hardcover)

DEDICATED TO

Everyone in the community of Richwood who has continued to keep this small village and its history alive.

History is a cyclic poem written by time upon the memories of man.

~Percy Bysshe Shelley

CONTENTS

PREFACE

The United States, along with Ohio, has been occupied and lived on long before Europeans came to settle the land. The natives of Ohio were known as the Hopewell culture. The Hopewell were an innovative and sophisticated culture built by a collection of tribes. Despite their differences, these tribes had one thing in common: they were engineers. This culture was known to build mounds. While they weren't the first mound builders, they certainly were one of the best. They specialized in geometric shapes like circles, squares and octagons with parallel lines connecting these shapes into a coherent complex. This culture emerged around 200 BC and started to die out circa 400 AD. The place that we call "Ohio" was the epicenter of this culture. Though the culture spread throughout the Great Lakes region and the Ohio and Mississippi valleys. We should also note that we don't know what these Indians called themselves. We use the name "Hopewell" only because artifacts relating to this culture were found in the late 19th century on a farm owned by a man whose last name was Hopewell.

We can't even use the term Ohio to describe the place where these Hopewell Indians lived. That's an invention of a later day. So how exactly did the Hopewell spread their influence throughout the eastern North Americas? The answer is the Hopewell Interaction Sphere. This sphere can be defined as a decentralized power structure that organizes diverse groups into a cohort system of cultural and technological exchange. It helps to contrast the interaction sphere with an empire. Pick any empire in the history of the world. In most empires, you see a large-scale military, bureaucracy collecting and spending taxes, powerful leaders guiding the agenda of this empire. They seek to impose its will on people.

But the interaction sphere had none of that. They spread their influence and prosperity by enticing people rather than coercing them. The first element of the Hopewell Interaction Sphere is the Mississippi River system. Remember at this time two thousand years ago that there are no cars, planes nor even horses in North America. To travel, you either had to go by foot or by water. Remember that the Hopewell Interaction Sphere had as its goal to spread prosperity and ideas and entice people to join in this collection of tribes and enrich each other's life. To do that, you have to travel. So, water is the first main element of the Hopewell Interaction Sphere.

Water leads to our next big element: exchange. The Hopewell's trading network nearly matched the Mississippi River system; that's not a coincidence. The items they exchanged also were not found in Ohio such as shark teeth, copper, knife river chert and silver. Also note that these items are luxuries, not necessities. This means that the Hopewell had a decision to make: Do we want to be self-sufficient? They could have fed and protected themselves without ever engaging the wider world; without ever taking the risk of talking to someone who didn't think or look like they did. They decided instead that they would be better off in dealing with strangers. But that meant having to offer something to these strangers. They instead participated in mutually beneficial specialization.

This idea should sound familiar to you. Our global trading network is much larger than the continental network that the Hopewell culture created. But the principle is the same. Both you today and the Hopewell two thousand years ago decided to take a risk to find out how strangers can enrich your life. Today, we rely on large, centralized organizations to make that process work. This includes private companies, national governments, international trade organizations, and even the U.S. military to make these processes work. But two thousand years ago, based out of a place that we call Ohio, the Hopewell managed this complicated process without large-scale coercive institutions. And they did so to acquire exotic materials not normally found in Ohio.

Take for example mica from western North Carolina. It is a brittle and fragile mineral that's not any good for making tools. It did, however, lend itself to delicate arts and crafts. How did they acquire these exotic materials? Technology. By technology, I quite literally mean mounds of dirt. The Newark Earthworks is perhaps the most significant of all the Hopewell mounds. The complex is located in Newark, Ohio and exists today as mainly circles and octagons. But the scale of this complex makes the wonders of the ancient world pale in comparison. Just one of the Giza pyramids fits in a small square at the complex and four coliseums in Rome fit into the octagon. The scale is remarkable precisely because the Hopewell had no urban centers. There was no density of population and they were a non-hierarchal society. So where did the labor come from and who did what and when and for how long? We have no idea.

But now we have to answer a pressing and related question: what does any of this have to do with technology? These piles of dirt are in reality a lunar observatory as it tracks the moon across the sky throughout its eighteen-and-a-half-year cycle. The moon at key moments in its journey lines up with openings in the octagon when the moon hits its most northerly extreme point. It lines up directly with the center of the octagon and the observatory circle. That's no easy feat. Scientists will tell you that tracking the motions of the moon are notoriously difficult. The Newark Earthworks combined both science and spirituality in the search for meaning.

So, what exactly happened to the Hopewell culture? If we look at the three things they did well—technology, exchange and religion—we see that around four or five hundred AD, something changed. For example, mound building declined, and the exchange network deteriorated. Ceremonies also subsided as pilgrims stopped coming to the place we call Ohio; they stopped seeking out that transformative scientific religious experience that the Newark Earthworks offered. We see an entirely new culture emerge in Ohio by 1000 AD. We call this culture the Fort Ancient culture. Though, as with the Hopewell, we have no idea what they really called themselves. It's interesting to note that this new culture had no clear genetic links to the Hopewell or their ancestors. In other words, the people of the Hopewell culture had disappeared, and we don't know what happened to them.

ACKNOWLEDGMENTS

There are a ton of people who contributed in numerous ways to this book. I first want to give a huge thanks to Charles Barry, one of our local historians. Many of these photographs were provided by him and those in the community. Without him, I'm certain much our history would've been lost.

A significant amount of information about Richwood was also taken from Bill Brown's "The Living Past... Roots of Richwood" articles from the Richwood Gazette. He did a ton of amazing research in the 1980s and collaborated with all of our knowledgeable citizens of Richwood. All of his articles and research is available to view in the local history room at the Richwood-North Union Public Library. Reddy Brown, son of Bill Brown, also helped immensely with his continued research. Please thank him and our amazing committee as they try to save our beloved Opera House.

I want to thank Barbara Holcomb, former president of the Carpe Diem Club, whose research into both the Club and the Richwood Public Library allowed that chapter to be written. Her investigations were very insightful and is a great addition to the history of Richwood. Barbara also wrote a history of the North Union Local School District with Jo Ann Stillings which greatly helped with that chapter as well.

I'd also like to give a special thanks to William "Russ" Coil, History professor at The Ohio State University. Without him, I wouldn't have had the plethora of information about Ohio and the changes the land had endured since the Hopewell Indians.

D. K. L.

Chapter 1

OHIO'S NATIVE BEGINNINGS

The story of how Ohio came to be, involves the most destructive warfare in North American history. Native Americans from Maryland to Illinois were forced to band together into mobile diverse communities with a shared interest in survival. They searched for places free of European diseases, intertribal warfare and even the effects of climate change. They sought to create independent communities far enough from the colonizing Europeans yet still close enough to trade with them. This catastrophic crisis began with germs. Far more Native Americans died in bed from Eurasian germs than on the battlefield from European guns and swords. After Christopher Columbus's arrival in 1492, the Indian population declined by as much as 95%. For Native Americans in the place that we call Ohio, that story has a twist.

Demographic crisis and community decline began decades before Native American-European contact in Ohio. This was due to trade routes and waterways which was the basic infrastructure that made the Hopewell Interaction Sphere work. It became a conduit for germs. As Indians fled the devastation of the coasts and Mississippi Valley, they fled along these ancient trade routes and carried with them germs. There was also violence such as the War of the Iroquois from the 1640s to the 1660s. It was perhaps considered the most widespread and destructive warfare in North American history. Most of the battles took place north of Lake Erie and played a strategic role. On the shores of Lake Erie, near what is now Cleveland, the Erie Nation were the only people standing in the way of the Iroquois and their complete control of the Great Lakes region. The Erie had bows and arrows while the Iroquois had guns. The battle was over in two years and by the 1680s, the Erie had all but disappeared as a nation.

The Iroquois claimed control over Ohio but never settled it. In fact, the territory south of Lake Erie became a war road, moving warriors east and west in a dangerous and violent thoroughfare. It was so violent that the rest of Ohio was depopulated until the early 18th century, around 1730. Many of the native refugees fled west to western refugee centers full of diverse languages and tribes. In 1701, the French and Indians who lived in the Great Lakes region managed to push back against the Iroquois, forcing peace. The Iroquois were forced to abandon their hunting territory west of Detroit. Peace meant that the refugee centers in the west could be abandoned as they moved back into fertile land and temperate climates once more, including the place that we call Ohio.

So, who settled here? A splinter group of the Huron, who originated in Ontario, Canada, resettled to Ohio and named themselves the Wyandot. Why did they change their name? In French, the word 'huron' meant rough person and they considered it an insult. Changing their name was a way of rejecting French authority. The Miamis also reestablished communities near French trading posts and along the Maumee and Wabash rivers. The Delawares, originally from Pennsylvania, also settled in eastern Ohio to escape the British and Iroquois. The Mingos, a splinter group from the Senecas, Cayugas, and refugees from Erie Nation and others, also settled in eastern Ohio from the mouth of Muskingum river to the Cuyahoga Valley. And of course, there were the Shawnees who settled along the Scioto Valley and later along the Miami and Mad Rivers in western Ohio.

By the 1730s and 1740s, these refugees had created an interesting world in the place of Ohio. It was full of villages and no clear cut tribally defined units. It was sainted villages of mixed ethnicities and languages. To the Native Americans, the diverse ethnic makeup of their villages was a defensive strategy. They figured that if an enemy knew that some relatives of theirs lived in that village, they wouldn't attack. This also meant that there was no one name for the land they now lived. What you called a river depended on who you were talking to and where.

So how did we get one name—Ohio—and not just any name but an Iroquois name? All of the Indians who lived in Ohio hated the Iroquois and rightly so. The Iroquois had brutalized their ancestors and not only that, but they claimed to control the land on which the Ohio Indians now live but in reality didn't. The truth of the matter is that they did so when it was convenient. The new refugee world meant a change in how Indians defined leadership. Instead of leaders with hereditary claims to power, refugee leadership meant accessing and redistributing wealth to the village.

Where did they find this wealth? They certainly could've been self-sufficient in 1750 but wealth to Native Americans in this time increasingly meant access to European goods. Leaders and villagers in Ohio had one responsibility: establish a village far enough away from Europeans that daily contact was difficult for safety and independence but close enough to trade with them. In the 1790s, American soldiers always remarked on one thing when they burned Ohio Indian villages down, their houses were solidly built and well furnished with silver cutlery, irons pots and other Western goods. So, Ohio Indians started to refer to it as the Ohio river because that's what the British wanted to call it and the British had adapted it from the Iroquois. In turn, the Ohio Indians adapted to the British because by 1750, the British increasingly had the better merchandise and cheaper prices compared to the French.

Ohio itself—both the river and the land—was invented to facilitate contact between Native Americans and Europeans. The French, in seeing that the Indians increasingly preferred the British, started to militarize the eastern border of the Ohio country—near what is now the border between Pennsylvania and Ohio. They built a series of forts stretching from Lake Erie down to modern-day Pittsburgh. The message to the English was: stay out. They also threatened the Indians themselves and pillaged a refugee town called

Pickawillany which was located along the Miami river in western Ohio. A man named Charles Langlade, who was of both French and Native American decent, took 250 Ottawa and Chippewa warriors to destroy the town in 1752.

The British colonists in Virginia and Pennsylvania decided to retaliate against French militarization. They wanted to send their own message to France: you can't keep us out. The colonists gathered together a militia consisting of British citizens and Iroquois allies. This militia was led by a young Virginian, the son of a wealthy planter. This young man had a life goal to be an officer in the British Army. There was only one problem, Virginia was considered to be a backwater. It was a place where nobody came from. To be an officer in the British military, you had to come from a well-connected London family. So, this mission provided the chance and the opportunity for the assignment to make a name for himself. The young Virginian was assigned to lead the troops to the frontier.

It was a dangerous mission going to the border between Pennsylvania and Ohio. The militia and their allies encountered French troops and skirmished. They even managed to capture the French officer in charge of the French unit. It was at this point that the young Virginian lost control of his soldiers. His Indian allies killed the French officer by splitting his skull and eating his brains. The young Virginian had witnessed and supervised a war crime and did nothing about it. Several other French soldiers were let go and they returned to their fort and told their story.

As a result, the French Army set out after the young Virginian and tracked him for several days to a clearing in the forest near Pittsburgh, Pennsylvania. When the French caught up with them, it was pouring rain and the British were exhausted. Their hastily built fort provided no protection from an overwhelming French firepower. To the young Virginian leader, the situation was clear: surrender or die. He surrendered, throwing himself at the mercy of the French. They would've had justification had they decided to kill him but instead they sent him home with a stern warning to stay out of Ohio. The date of that surrender was July 4th, 1785 and the young Virginian leader whose life was saved by the French that day was none other than George Washington.

This situation was what triggered the French and Indian War which lasted from 1754 to 1763. It was, in fact, the first global war in human history and it started over a fight about Ohio. The Indian towns in Ohio had rebelled against the French monarchy while being aided by the British. The French tried to stop these rebels, mainly through intimidation and later escalating into violent acts. The English used Washington's frontier stumble to declare war and continue their long struggle for global domination against their French rivals. Ohio Indians had to ask themselves who they wanted to ally with during this war. The answer was seemingly the French since they had a more powerful military and they also weren't interested in settling Ohio like the British were. They believed supporting the French was the best bet to support their goal of an Ohio free of European control. Unfortunately, they were wrong.

The British spent a fortune to defeat the French and in 1763, the British managed to force the French to surrender. They went bankrupt as a result but were able to evict the French from North America and gained control all the way to the Mississippi River. This was a stinging defeat for the French and one they would not soon forget. What happened to Ohio as a result? Indian villages were in decline due to starvation and Indians themselves were lost, both physically and spiritually. After the French and Indian War, the British believed they could dictate to the Indians. But they were also bankrupt and couldn't afford to deploy soldiers to their newly acquired land. Pontiac, an Ottawa warrior and leader, led the Native Americans to a rebellion against the king of England. They demanded to be treated as equals within the Empire. Pontiac's Rebellion lasted for about a year and resulted in the fall of Fort Sandusky in 1763. The British fort was situated along Sandusky Bay on Lake Erie.

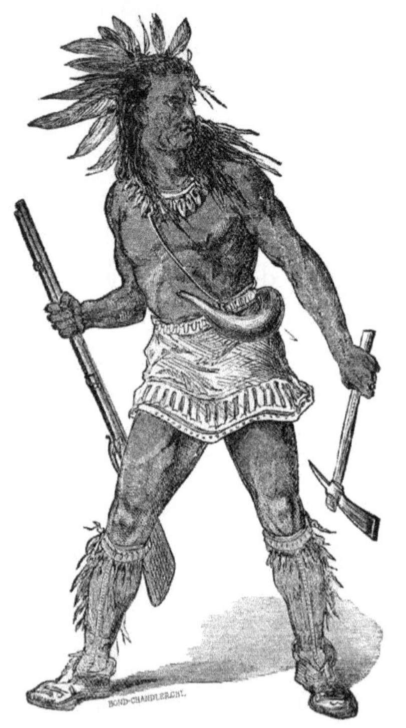

Pontiac, the Ottawa Warrior. Illustration contained in Beer's History of Union County, 1883.

This victory highlighted the problem that the British couldn't afford to protect their new lands. There were only 13 soldiers at Fort Sandusky which was easy pickings for Pontiac and his warriors. The British were forced to concede that they had to negotiate with the Indians of Ohio rather than dictate to them. In 1764, the Native American rebellion ended, and the British American rebellion started. In December of 1773, we see the most famous pre-revolutionary war protest when British colonists dressed as Indians and dumped tea into the Boston Harbor. Why did they dress as Indians? They wanted to connect, in a dramatic fashion, their struggle to a group of people who successfully forced the British in London to renegotiate the price of staying within the Empire.

This also started to raise tensions between white settlers and the Native Americans. The Proclamation Line of 1763 was a boundary that the British created along the Appalachian Mountains. It prohibited colonists from settling lands west of the line to appease the Native Americans. Around 1773, many settlers ignored the Proclamation Line and moved into the lands of the Indians. A cycle of violence and revenge ensued as white settlers murdered Indian women and children and Indians responded in kind to exact revenge. Virginian politicians and land speculators took advantage of the fragile situation and sent a couple thousand soldiers to gain control of the territory south of the Ohio River.

They met the Indian resistance at Point Pleasant with the Indians being badly defeated due to being outnumbered. The Indians were forced to cede territory south of the Ohio River to white settlers. The significance of this meant that for the first time the Ohio River became a border. We don't need to go into all the details of the American Revolution as I'm sure you know who ended up winning. But if we ask who won Ohio, the answer is less clear-cut. I ask instead: when did the violence actually end? The answer, of course, is that it didn't until the 1790s. An example of this was the Massacre at Gnadenhutten in March of 1782. Gnadenhutten is located in eastern Ohio along the Tuscarawas River.

In 1781, the British forced the Delaware Indians who lived there to abandon their community as the British could no longer protect them against attacks from whites in Pennsylvania. The British moved the Delaware Indians to the Sandusky area up near Lake Erie but the Indians arrived too late in their new home to plant crops and so they faced serious food shortages in the winter of 1781 and 1782. In the early spring of 1782, a small group returned to Gnadenhutten to harvest whatever food was left. Meanwhile, a group of Pennsylvania militiamen we're looking for a raiding party responsible for recent attacks in Pennsylvania. They happened upon Gnadenhutten and saw that the Delaware Indians there had western-style clothes and owned pewter tea sets and pewter cutlery.

The Pennsylvania militia concluded that the Indians must have stolen these items because everyone knew that Indians ate only with wooden bowls and spoons and wore clothes only made by hand in Indian villages. They knew too that only Christian civilized people owned these kinds of things and Indians, by definition, could not be civilized or Christian and so the militia blamed the Delaware Indians for the raids. They separated the group by gender, put them in two different buildings and made them sleep there overnight. In the morning, however, they took these Indians two-by-two to a slaughterhouse, stunned them with mallet blows to the head and then fatally scalped them, killing 28 men, 29 women, and 39 children. All this because Indians weren't supposed to own western-style goods. What a tragic way to deny the very reason for Ohio's invention.

Chapter 2

WHITE SETTLEMENT OF OHIO

After the American Revolution, eastern elites like George Washington and Thomas Jefferson viewed Ohio with a mixture of suspicion and hope. They hoped that Ohio could, in theory, provide inexpensive land for ordinary Americans and an opportunity for individuals to own land and be free. They also suspected that Ohio presented several problems for the new nation. First, George Washington feared Ohio would be disconnected from the east. His main concern was the Appalachian Mountains as to him they were considered a barrier separating Americans from one another. People west of the Appalachians, Washington feared, would slowly become loyal to other countries if they offered the people something the U.S. couldn't. Elites were also concerned that the wrong people were moving to Ohio.

In 1784, the national government sent Colonel Josiah Harmar to Ohio with troops to prevent and discourage squatters. Squatters were people living on and working land to which they had no legal title. Harmar set up shop where the Muskingum meets the Ohio River. He did what he could to discourage squatters by burning their crops, tearing down their cabins and jailing violators. Despite this, people kept coming anyway. Even after the U.S. Military defeated the Ohio Indians, that world lingered and upsetting the social and racial norms of eastern elites.

One village, in particular, greatly confused eastern elites. It was called Negro town, located just to the north of Upper Sandusky. For years before the American Revolution, it was a Wyandot Indian village. In the 1790s, documents suggested a free black man lived there too. He worked as a trader and moved back and forth between Detroit where he would get his supplies and this and other Wyandot villages. He also had a partner who was a Wyandot Indian.

After 1794, when the U.S. defeated the Ohio Indians at Fallen Timbers, the Wyandot slowly began moving westward but a few people stayed in this village, especially several black families who had moved there from Detroit. How did Negro town get its name? We can't know for certain but in 1808, five years after Ohio became a state, a Christian missionary traveled to Detroit by crossing Ohio to reach the Maumee River and then Lake Erie. He wrote of a village south of Lake Erie that had once been an old Wyandot town and in an 1808 letter, the missionary called it Negro town. That's the first documented use of the name. The missionary estimated that around six or seven African American families lived there and here's how he describes them: "They have been among the Indians for a long time and have taken their way of life."

Why was Negro town so confusing to eastern elites? By the late 1790s, this village was black, Indian and mixed-race and it was by culture too. Its residents drew on African and Indian traditions to create lives of their own choosing. It was also clearly aligned with the British and French-Canadian settlers who remained in Detroit after the U.S. took control after the American Revolution. Just as unsettling, this community helped slaves who lived in Detroit during the south to escape to freedom in 1803. In fact, there were reportedly 40 black families who lived there. What we find is an unusual place in Ohio; a place of freedom for marginalized people, blacks and Indians who made their own rules. Eastern elites couldn't quite trust that.

To address their fears, eastern elites created a model town, one they hoped would be the future of Ohio. They called it Marietta. The town has its origins in a real estate deal in 1787. The Ohio Company of Associates, a private company seeking to profit from land speculation, purchased 1.5 million acres in southeastern Ohio, along the Ohio River. They bought it from the national government, the owners of the land who intended to use proceeds from the sale to pay off Revolutionary War debt. At the very least it was an investment group, but it was also a collection of like-minded patriotic activists. The company's leaders were men who served as officers in the American Revolution. In addition to turning a profit, they saw their job as succeeding where France and Great Britain had stumbled; moving people to the west and building towns that advanced the American cause.

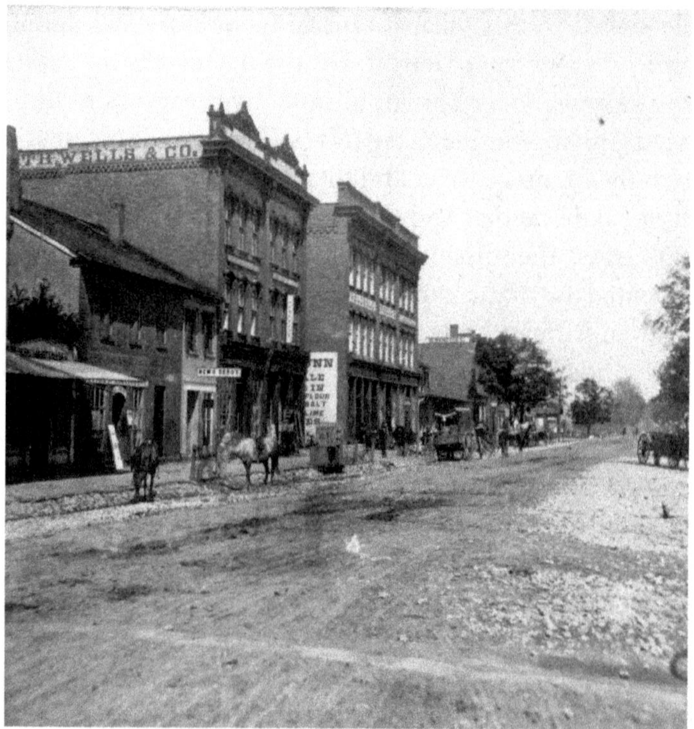

Marietta, Front Street circa 1850-1859.

Marietta was built close to where Col. Josiah Harmar established his fort. It's important to think about that location as the landscape was mainly the foothills of the Appalachian Mountains. This rough, rocky terrain was not good for farming and, therefore, it attracted mainly hunters and subsistence farmers. Plus, the Muskingum was prone to flooding at certain times of the year and is very shallow at other times. In other words, it tends to be an unreliable transportation system. But the forests in the area were thick with old-growth trees that were ideal for, among other things, shipbuilding. So lumber was a crucial natural resource for Marietta and one that influenced the development of the town's early economy.

Marietta was also designed to specifically create dutiful, responsible, and patriotic American citizens. Physical space mattered because it could shape individual behavior. Most of the planning took place in Boston in 1787, far from the actual location. A few of the leaders did visit Marietta and they took care to note special local features. For example, they were impressed by the large conical shape Indian Mound at the center of the town. They preserved it and made it the center of their town cemetery. However, this plan imposed on the local area rather than worked with it.

The town adopted a strict gridiron layout, making it predictable which suggested order and rules rather than spontaneity which was disorderly and chaotic. Streets, according to the plan, had to be 100 feet wide. On the side of the streets, the town had to plant trees and not just any trees but mulberry trees. These trees would be planted ten feet from the houses that lined the streets. The streets themselves took on names in order to reinforce the sense of public duty in the town's residents. They named streets after famous Americans and the town's patriotic founders. Of course, there would also be churches and schools everywhere. You needed institutions that taught people how to behave.

So eastern elites wanted Marietta to be led by Revolutionary War veterans. They wanted an orderly, tight-knit, predictable and nurturing settlement that connected to the wider world. So how did the state of Ohio develop along the lines of Marietta and the goal of the town's founders? As it turns out, the state of Ohio developed as a diverse, mobile and profit-seeking population and it developed in an unpredictable chaotic fashion. This was mainly because the state of Ohio was born in an age of rapid technological change.

In particular, it was steam power like steamboats but also railroads as well. And wherever you had railroads, you had the Telegraph to send information instantaneously across long distances. These new technologies facilitated global migration. From 1830 to 1930, 90 million global migrants moved around the world which was the most in human history. It appears that steam power, which was so eagerly awaited by the leaders of Marietta, actually undermined their vision of a tightly knit like-minded stable community. Steam power moved people and ideas as much as it moved goods.

The steamboat enabled faster, cheaper and more flexible travel. For example, if you wanted to travel upriver from New Orleans to Louisville in 1817, that trip took 25 days. By 1826, you were down to eight days. The railroad also improved upon the steamboat's flexibility and power. You could finally take a railroad trip across the Appalachian Mountains from Cleveland to New York City. By 1850, that trip took just 24 hours. Remember in 1784, George Washington wanted more than anything else to eliminate those mountains as a barrier separating the east and the west. The railroad did that and you got faster, and cheaper information flows as well. Consider the length it would take a letter or a newspaper to travel from New York City to Cincinnati. In 1817, that trip took 19 days. In 1840, that same trip took ten days and in 1850, thanks to the Telegraph, that trip was now instantaneous. We shouldn't be surprised that Ohio was resettled and rebuilt by a variety of people from a variety of places. More heads of households in Ohio had been born in foreign countries than were born in Ohio. That's a remarkable statement and I think it means that technological change opened Ohio to the world with a greater speed and intensity than ever before. The vision of Marietta's founders could not withstand that kind of change.

Chapter 3

CREATION OF CLAIBOURNE TOWNSHIP

The state of Ohio as we know it was admitted to the Union on March 1, 1803. The Legislature wanted a state formed as soon as possible and succeeded in getting Congress to pass an act, April 30, 1802, authorizing the calling of a constitutional convention. The enabling act provided for an election of delegates to the constitutional convention to be held in September of 1802. The thirty-five delegates met at Chillicothe on the first Monday of the following November. By a vote of thirty-four to one, the negative vote being cast by Ephraim Cutler, the delegation decided to proceed to the organization of a state government and the formation of a constitution. The convention was in session until November 29th, at which time it had completed the first constitution for the state and the one which lasted until 1851, when a second constitution was adopted.

When the Ordinance of 1787 was formally put into operation, on July 17, 1788, the capital was established at Marietta. The ordinance became the foundation of the constitution of the future state of Ohio. The capital remained at Marietta until 1800, when it was moved by the congressional act of May 7th of that year to Chillicothe and by the constitution adopted in 1802 the capital was to remain there until 1808. The Legislature of 1809 moved the capital to

Zanesville until a permanent site could be selected. The War of 1812 made it necessary to move the capital back to Chillicothe, where there was less danger from attack by the Indians and the British. Commissioners appointed by the Legislature had selected a small village called Dublin to be the capital but was later rejected by the Legislature. The capital was permanently located at Columbus by the legislative act of February 14, 1812. Nine total sites were under consideration before the decision was made.

The move to Columbus was spurred because of pressure to move the capital to a central location. The Ohio General Assembly chose the Forks of the Scioto at a place known as "Wolf's Ridge". The legislature was offered 10 acres for the statehouse and 10 more for a penitentiary and other buildings. The town then came to be known as Columbus thanks to the lobbying efforts of Joseph Foos, a local legislator. North of the Statehouse Square, along High Street, was the state and federal courthouse. The square was mostly a cornfield which was tended to by the first mayor of Columbus. The rest of the town remained a dense forest of various native trees. Ponds and natural springs littered the area which connected to creeks that ran into the Scioto river. In April of 1812, various signs advertised the new town and encouraged land sales mostly near High Street.

Columbus had about 700 people in the early 1800's and was filled with local stores and taverns. The city became the capital of Ohio only five years after President James Monroe visited. His visit, however, wasn't spurred because of leisure; he was on a mission to strengthen America's military. Federalists disliked the War of 1812 and Monroe hoped to tour the northern states to survey the country's coastal defenses and help end partisan divisions. On his way back from Detroit, the president was met in Worthington by the Franklin Dragoons. He was escorted to Columbus in August of 1817 and gave speeches at the Ohio Statehouse. He complimented the city, referring to it as an "infant city", and admired the prospects for the town in the future.

Union county was formed from Franklin, Delaware, Logan and Madison counties in 1820. Col. James Curry, a member of the state legislature, was the chief instigator of the formation of the county. The Ewing brothers made the first settlement in 1798. Curry submitted an act to erect the county of Union which was passed on January 10, 1820. The boundaries were drawn which included the northern part of the county bordering the Greenville line. The treaty of Greenville was written in 1795 which essentially separated Ohio in half. The northern part of the state was occupied by the Wyandot, Delaware, Shawnee, Ottawa, Miami, Eel River, Wea, Chippewa, Potawatomi, Kickapoo, Piankashaw, and Kaskaskia nations. White settlers claimed the land south of the treaty line. Indians were still allowed to hunt on the land that they ceded. The treaty was "updated" in 1814, after the War of 1812, which urged peace between the U.S. and the Wyandots, Delawares, Shawanoese, Senacas and Miamies as well as an alliance between these tribes.

When Union county was organized, three subdivisions included the townships of Union, Darby and Mill Creek. Other townships weren't formed until a few years after the formation of Union county. Claibourne township was formed on March 5, 1833 from the south part of Jackson township. York township was set off on December 3, 1822 before the organization of Claibourne. Washington township was formed from York township on June 9, 1836 lying north of the Greenville treaty line. Two towns existed in Claibourne township, Richwood and Claibourne.

A man named Cyprian Lee petitioned to have the township of Jackson divided into two townships; the southern part was to be called Claibourne and the northern part retaining the name Jackson. It was ordered by the County Commissioners on March 5, 1834 that Levi Phelps was to begin laying out the township of Claibourne. Cyprian Lee is accredited with being the first settler of Claiborne township. The exact date of his settlement is unknown, though it was reportedly sometime between 1820 and 1825. His was the first cabin built west of the Scioto River in the region and stood several miles south of Richwood on the south bank of Fulton Creek. The next three settlers were Edward "Ned" Williams, Robert Cotrell and Henry Swartz. Each of them purchased land from Lee and settled as his neighbors.

Indian tribes had previously used Claibourne township as hunting grounds until white settlers started to colonize the area. The site of Richwood was rich, not only in trees, but in game as well. The

Indians often tented on these grounds which is established by the fact that many past relics have been found in the vicinity. Knives, Indian saddle fragments, tomahawks, brooches and even skeletons have all been found.

After the white settlers had occupied the area of northern Union county, the forests were full of hunters by both pioneers and the Indians. The Native Americans would not tolerate the presence of white settlers north of the Greenville line, but they frequently hunted south of the line as they were allowed as outlined in the treaty. While feelings between the two weren't the best, amicable relations were maintained. Indians, sometime due to retaliation of aggression, would occasionally shoot the settler's hogs as they fed in the woods. It was a custom for the white pioneers to mark a tree that contained bees to indicate that they claimed the tree and therefore the honey that it contained. Indians didn't do this and harvested the honey despite any initials carved into the tree; this tended to anger the white settlers. Despite this, Indians would often visit the cabins of settlers and eat with them. They would also engage in foot races and other kinds of games.

One story in the area proclaims that two of Claibourne Township's earliest settlers, Ned Williams and Henry Swartz, had killed two Indians along Peacock Run in the southern part of Claibourne township. While it was never proved, the missing Indians were never heard from again and the evidence strongly suggested that these two had killed them. Swartz, who fought in the War of 1812, was known for having a fiery temper which he would often take out on the Indians of the area. On one occasion, he beat one of them with a ramrod of his gun. He would also sneak into their camps and play annoying tricks. The Indians sought out Swartz in reconciliation, but the pioneer gave them no satisfaction.

A nearby Indian camp erected sticks with bullets on the ends around their land to indicate war. Soon after this, two of their comrades had gone hunting and didn't return. The Indians diligently searched for them but to no avail. Suspecting foul play, they traced the men to Peacock Run, but found no indication of their presence beyond that. Captain Henry Swartz and Ned Williams had been clearing land and burning brush in the vicinity and the Indians suspected them. They visited Swartz's cabin and the man was apparently unconcerned but watchful. The Indians wished to be friendly and wanted to borrow his gun to shoot targets with him, but he refused.

One day, an old Indian hunter came to his place and proposed a hunt. Swartz agreed and insisted that the Indian hunter lead. They hunted for a long time, both men watching each other more closely than the deer they were hunting. Finally, the Indian proposed that they split up; Swartz insisted that he take the side closer to home. After they separated, and the Indian was out of sight, Swartz turned and hastily ran home. The Indian followed and yelled at the man that he lied. Swartz, with a discharge still remaining in his rifle, pointed his weapon at the Indian. The hunter made no further attempt and swiftly departed. Afterward, Swartz was always weary when he believed Indians were nearby. Soon afterward, the Indians withdrew permanently from the region.

Swartz, when asked about this story, would never admit to it one way or another. He neither denied nor admitted to killing or knowing of the deaths of the two Indians. There was a well-beaten path along the bank of Peacock Run by the side of which stood an old sycamore tree, from which had fallen a large limb, sinking deep in the ground. This was near the place where Swartz and Williams had been clearing and around the limb a large fire was made. After a fall of snow, Zach Stephens, a brother-in-law of Henry Swartz, while hunting for some lost cattle, stepped into the hole made by the limb. He fell, and on withdrawing his foot, found the lower jawbone of a human stuck to the sole of his boot. Suspecting how it got there, he traveled to Swartz's cabin and asked if he knew anything about it. Swartz's face reportedly grew pale upon seeing the bone but made no response. It was believed that both he and Williams had killed the two Indians and buried their remains.

Chapter 4

FOUNDING OF RICHWOOD

Richwood, located in what became Claibourne township one year later, was laid out in August of 1832 by Philip Plummer. The town is on Pelham survey No. 6,307, which was long known as the "rich woods." Plummer had come into possession of the William Pelham Survey of 1,200 acres and visited it in the summer of 1832 from Mount Vernon, Knox county, Ohio; with him was his brother, Thomas Plummer, Elisha Merriot and Dr. John P. Brookins, a physician searching for a place to practice medicine. They traveled in a large two-horse wagon and stopped on the way at a house owned by a man named Daniel Swartz located along the Scioto River. The village was surveyed and platted on August 8, 9 and 10, 1832 by Thomas G. Plummer, Special Deputy Surveyor, and Levi Phelps, County Surveyor. The plat was acknowledged before Ira Wood, Justice of the Peace, on August 20, 1832. They all returned to Mount Vernon until such time as Philip Plummer and Dr. Brookins traveled back to Richwood to build cabins for themselves and their families.

The first work after their arrival was to build a little shanty for shelter, a place to stay and a general headquarters while surveying and preparing houses. The shanty was small and was covered with brush and blankets. 1832 was the year of the pestilence of cholera in

Ohio, and Mr. Thomas Plummer had prepared before leaving Mt. Vernon a bottle of "cholera catch-up," the principal ingredient of which was cayenne pepper. The camp was named "Camp Catch-up," and was the only thing for shelter for miles around.

Cholera was considered an emerging disease in the 19th century, meaning it existed in specific and local places long before the 19th century but emerged as a global disease during the 1800s. It was also considered the great scourge in the 19th century, meaning other diseases killed more people but cholera took you from health to death in a matter of hours. Victims also suffered from violent purges that left them dehydrated and left their system lacking oxygen which means their extremities went into gangrene. Cholera was transmitted from what doctors call the oral-fecal route. In other words, humans drank water tainted with feces.

Cholera has its origins in the Ganges River Delta in India. In 1817, an outbreak escaped its local confines and by 1831, had reached Western Europe and by 1832, North America. The disease moved through migration and trade. The ability of people to move farther and faster than ever before also allowed their diseases to travel farther and faster than ever before. Technology aided the spread of cholera and so it's a perfect fit for Ohio because Ohio was created by the same forces that created cholera, the global disease. Ohio's water routes opened Ohio to the world's people. Not just their ideas and goods, but their germs as well.

Before the Civil War in the United States, there were two major cholera epidemics in Cincinnati from 1832 to 1833. 1,000 people died and that's with a total population in Cincinnati of 24,000 people. From 1849 to 1851, 8,000 people died in Cincinnati and that was with a population of 115,000 people. By comparison, New York City lost 5,000 people with a population of 515,000 people. Cholera, therefore, thrived in places characterized by rapid unplanned urbanization and societies affected by gross inequalities of wealth.

The first cabin in Richwood was occupied by Dr. John P. Brookins and family, consisting of the Doctor and Mrs. Brookins, Miss Jane Coffey, niece of the Doctor, their little daughter, Jane Mary and a boy who lived with them, W.H. Frank. The cabin, a one-room building, was built on the north side of Ottawa Street. The cabin was one story high with the logs scutched inside and out, clapboard roof and puncheon floor with openings for a door without a screen and two windows without sash or glass with no chinking or daubing between the logs. A great fireplace took up a large portion of the west end of the cabin. The back and ends of the fireplace were built out of wood and mud; the chimney was made out of sticks plastered inside and out with mud.

A short time after Dr. Brookins moved into his cabin, Absalom Carney built himself a cabin on the corner of East Bomford and Franklin Streets, near the center of the surveyed town plat. His was the second one in town. Mr. Carney was a blacksmith, but the only business he had for now was to upset and sharpen the axe and grubbing hoe since they were about the only instruments in town. But Mr. Carney, with the rest, had faith and hope and perseverance. He found business all the time in clearing up his lot and building his cabin for the winter. He was a fine man and like the others, very industrious. Absalom later moved west to Barry County, Missouri where he was killed by Native Americans in January of 1892. He was 59 years old at the time of his death.

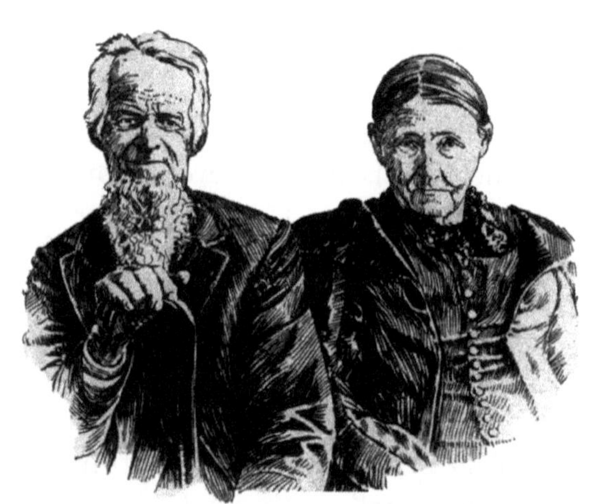

Illustration of W.H. Frank, 80, and Rachael Frank, his wife, appearing in the Richwood Gazette on Aug. 12, 1897.

The boy, W.H. Frank, built the third cabin for a home for his widowed mother. Frank's father had died when he was 7 years of age. The boy lived with Mr. Baker Plummer, the second brother of Phillip Plummer, when he was 10 years old. The man owned a hotel, called the Stage House, in Mt. Vernon. W.H. Frank worked for him as a chore boy and carefully saved up the money he earned. He later went to live with Dr. John P. Brookins as a recommendation from Mr. Baker. Frank lived with the Doctor and his family and came with him to Richwood in 1832. Frank bought a lot from Philip Plummer and talked with him about building his own cabin. A man named Andrew, who lived 2 miles southwest of Richwood on Fulton Creek, helped the boy by building his cabin in exchange for Frank's watch, his pig, which Frank also bought from Philip Plummer, and a little sum of money. Frank later moved to Marysville, Ohio where he married his wife, Rachael. They moved to Romeyn, Nebraska where they spent the rest of their life together. W.H. and Rachael were married for 60 years as of 1897.

The fourth cabin was built by a Mr. Evans, who engaged in making shoe-maker's lasts for boots and shoes. There was plenty of good timber on his own town lot and anywhere in the streets and alleys of Richwood. He was a clever and industrious man and had no family. He was the only businessman in town that brought any return for his labor. He would send them to various towns and cities, most of them to Dayton, Ohio. It was a good place for his business, so far as manufacturing was concerned. His expenses were not much, and material costed nothing except the timber, and it was right at his door. He had no machinery except a workbench and various knives.

The first death occurred in Richwood one year after settlement. Jane Mary, the little daughter and only child at that time of Dr. and Mrs. Brookins, was playing with her cousins, William and John Woods, and each one had a fire. Jane Mary's was burning well, but the boys could not get theirs to burn, and they asked her to make them burn. She took her apron to fan the fire and sat down over some coals that had scattered, and her clothing took fire from them. Before help could reach her, she was so badly burned that she died a few hours later. Henry Swartz, who was near the area at the time, presumably burned his hands in trying to extinguish the fire. Philip Plummer helped to clear off the ground and dig the grave for said child. She is currently buried in the Old Richwood Cemetery on Ottawa Street behind the Richwood Chapel.

The first store was opened at Richwood in a little log building which stood on lot 102. It was owned by men named Burdick and

Callaway in August 1833. Hezekiah Burdick was a local Methodist Episcopal preacher and had owned and cultivated a small farm three miles southeast from Marysville, on Mill Creek. John Callaway was born at the Scioto Salt Works in what is now Jackson County in 1802 where his father was engaged in making salt. A year or two later they removed to Yellow Springs in Greene County where Mr. Calloway was a proprietor of a Tavern for two years. He then entered a half-section of land in that county and, after occupying it for eight years, was defrauded of it by a process of legal deception. He then moved to Clark county and from that county young John went to Marysville to try his fortunes there. He became owner of a small property near Marysville and two town lots.

Misters Burdick and Callaway purchased a small stock of goods at Marysville owned by L.H. Hastings and moved them to Richwood. The stock embraced a few staple groceries and dry goods, and the entire amount was conveyed to Richwood in one load. As both the purchasers were inexperienced in merchandising, it was stipulated in the contract of sale that Mr. Hasting should remain with them several weeks until Mr. Callaway could become accustomed to his position behind the counter. This store remained in operation about two years. Mr. Callaway withdrew and soon after, Mr. Burdick closed out his entire stock. Financially, the first store was not a brilliant success. Mr. Burdick soon removed to other parts but Major John Callaway, as he was universally known, took unto himself a wife, Clarky R. Tonguet, in 1835 and settled down to rustic life near Richwood. The store later became Ferrier's Saddlery Shop.

The growth of Richwood for many years was extremely slow, there were many obstacles to impede its progress, and discourage settlers situated many miles from any market. In the midst of a sparsely settled region of country, it is not surprising that Mr. Plummer should have his hands full in keeping his little colony together; and, notwithstanding all his efforts and liberality, many became discouraged, and either sought some more favorable locality or returned to their old homes in the eastern portion of the state.

Many annoyances and inconveniences were to be submitted to. The mails, for instance, put in an appearance quite infrequently, and were carried on horseback by Mr. Plummer or some of his neighbors. Dr. Brookins was the first Post-master, which office he held for many years; and during all his official life, he never permitted Uncle Sam's mail beg to depart empty. The markets were also distantly located. Farmers were compelled to haul their grain to Toledo and Sandusky for a market and then receiving but a mere pittance for the same. But notwithstanding all these drawbacks, the town moved slowly but surely onward.

The completion of the Atlantic & Great Western Railroad was an important era in the history of the town. It increased in value every acre of land in the county and gave to the place a renewed impetus of growth. It opened up new and previously unapproachable markets and was, in every respect, a consideration that had been long and devoutly wished. The railroad eventually became known as the Erie Railroad which was chartered in 1851. It ran through the county from northeast to southwest, having station points at Woodland, Richwood, Claibourne, Broadway, Peoria and Pottersburg.

Richwood was incorporated as a village by the County Commissioners on March 6, 1855 by reason of a petition from forty-one citizens of Richwood. This action was taken by the citizens of Richwood in anticipation for the Atlantic & Great Western Railroad. Charles W. Rosette was elected Mayor in 1855 and re-elected in 1856 and 1857. The incorporation lapsed or became dormant for a time until B.W. Hayes was elected Mayor in 1864.

The Richwood Planing Mill, under the proprietorship of S. Carter & Co., was an enterprise of importance to the town and it deserves an extended description in this connection. Established in 1871, it had taken a front rank among the leading manufacturing enterprises in the county and was considered one of the best Planing Mills in the state. The proprietorship comprises Misters Carter, A.J. Blake and S.M. Blake, three of Richwood's leading businessmen as the time. The mill was equipped with first class machinery and was supplied with all the latest improvements. The establishment furnished employment from five to seven hands and was an important addition to Richwood.

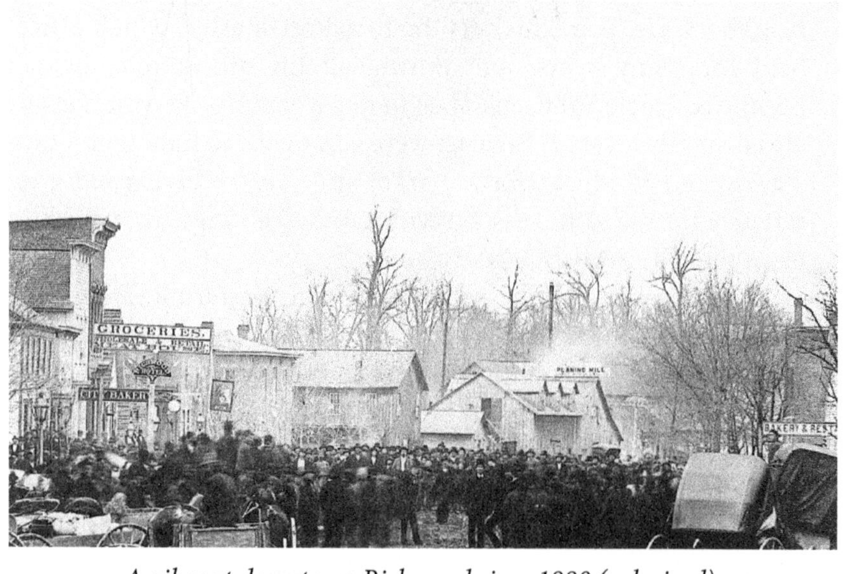

A vibrant downtown Richwood circa 1880 (colorized).

Other manufacturing businesses in Richwood included: The Richwood Flouring Mills, under the proprietorship of G.W. Cannan, the Richwood Woolen Mills, owned by Loveless & Howe, Tucker Bros., who manufactured wagons and carriages, and R. Ferrier's Saddlery Shop, who manufactured harness and saddlery for horses. The Bank of Richwood was also an enterprise of great importance and one that continues today. The bank was established in 1867 by G.B. Hamilton as president. The stock first amounted to around $20,000. They represented an aggregate capital of $140,000 by 1875. At that time, it was under the management of W.H. Conkright as President & B.L. Talmage as Cashier. In total, there were approximately 38 various businesses and warehouses including three banks and three newspapers in the town of Richwood by the 1880s.

The Corporation of Richwood owned an engine house which was built in 1875 at the cost of about $1,300 and had a fire department. A destructive fire occurred on Friday evening April 9th, 1875 on the East side of Franklin Street between Blagrove and Ottawa Streets. It was discovered in a barn at the rear of Westheimer's Dry Goods and Grocery Store, and soon the frame hardware store of Godmen, Thornhill and Co., across the alley, took fire; a barn farther to the east, at the rear of the Methodist Protestant church, caught fire as well which took the church with it. Telegrams for help were sent to Urbana and Marion with the latter responded by sending a hand engine. But before it could arrive, the flames were already extinguished. Nine buildings in total were destroyed in all with a loss amounting to more than $25,000. Although the council had previously taken action looking to establish a fire department, this destructive fire caused them to push it to completion with greater vigor than before.

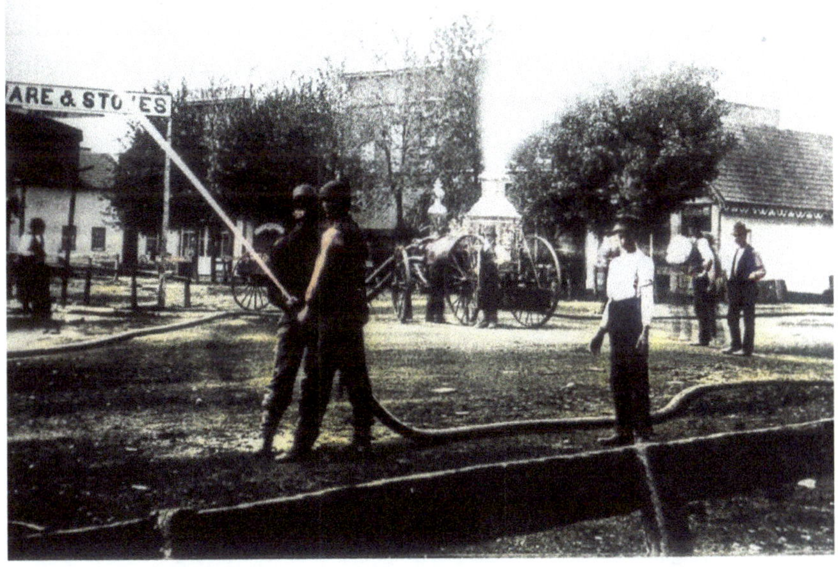

Demonstration of the newly purchased steam engine circa 1875 (colorized).

A hook and ladder company composed of 30 members was organized in May of 1875 with Colonel W.L. Curry as Captain. The council had previously purchased a few hooks and ladders and had ordered a wagon made. A steam engine was ordered directly after the fire had occurred from Silsbee & Co. in Seneca Falls, New York and was received on June 11th, 1875. It, with the hose cart and 800 feet of hose, costed $5,250. The hose company and engine company were organized in June of 1875 and J.S. Gill was elected engineer. The fire department was a volunteer organization until 1881 when the council organized three departments. The hook and ladder company consisted of nine members with N.W. Spratt as foreman.

The hose company contained 9 men and had V.F. Collier for its foreman. W.S. Bowers was foreman of the engine company which had seven members. The members of the department were paid for all services rendered either during fires or while on drill. Scattered over the village were 8 cluster wells each with 14 to 20 branches driven into the ground about 21 or 22 feet. The branches centered in a 5-inch hydrant and the water supply from them was regarded as inexhaustible. The wells costed about $350 each. W.W. Kile was the first chief of the Department. He served two years and was exceeded for one year by O. Curry. George B. Tucker was then elected chief by the company in 1879 and when the department was reorganized by the council, he was appointed to this position and held it for numerous years.

Chapter 5

THE CIVIL WAR

During the 1830s, Ohioans had slowly begun to change their minds about who they were. Increasingly that meant rejecting the pan-Mississippian world that they had done so much to create. It meant imagining the Ohio River in a new way as a border between two groups of white people. On one side of the border, there was a morally superior civilization valuing hard work and freedom. On the other side of the border was a degraded and backward people, a morally inferior people because of the presence of slavery. To make this new attitude work, Ohioans had to refocus their state to the east across the Appalachians.

Our story begins not in Ohio but in New York with the building of the Erie Canal. Built between 1817 and 1825, the original Erie Canal traversed 363 miles. It was the longest artificial waterway and the greatest public works project in North America. It transported goods and people across the northern part of New York back and forth from Buffalo and Lake Erie in the West to Albany in the Hudson River in the East. Before the Erie Canal, that trip took two weeks. After the Erie Canal was built, it took five days. The price of transport also fell by 90 percent.

The Erie Canal put New York on the map as the Empire State. It became the leader in the nation in population, industry, and economic strength. Of course, everyone's real goal was to reach New York City, not Albany, but that merely required a trip down the Hudson River to New York City and it's ocean port. Because of the Erie Canal, New York City became the nation's principal port, the nation's most populous city, and the nation's foremost seat of commerce and finance. If only Ohioans could find a way to connect to New York's Erie Canal and get their goods quickly to Lake Erie so that they need not cross the cumbersome Appalachian Mountains or sail down the Ohio to the Mississippi to New Orleans. New York was where Ohioans wanted to be. If only, in other words, Ohioans had their own canal that connected the southern part of the state, it's most populated and economically developed part, to Lake Erie, it's least populated and least economically developed part.

In 1825, the state of Ohio started construction on the Ohio and Erie Canal which took seven years to build. When completed, the canal was 308 miles long connecting Portsmouth on the Ohio River to Cleveland on Lake Erie. When Ohio began construction, the governor of New York and the governor of Ohio met near Newark, Ohio to dig the first hole. They faced east when they dug their shovels into the ground to symbolize the beginning of a change. Ohioans would no longer look west and south toward New Orleans but increasingly they would look east to New York City. Miami Canal took longer in part because of funding issues but when completed, it was 245 miles long and connected Cincinnati and Toledo. Now both the eastern and western parts of the state were connected from north to south, from river to lake.

How did the canals change the state of Ohio? First, the northern third of the state began to grow in terms of both population and economic activity. An Akron farmer saw the price of wheat doubling. After the Ohio and Erie Canal was completed, they could now meet growing demand in eastern cities for western wheat. In Toledo, the value of trade activity increased from 8 million dollars in 1840 to 31 million dollars in 1850 and in the little town of Milan, best known as the birthplace of Thomas Edison, became for a few years in the late 1840s the second largest grain port in the world behind only Odessa, Russia. Cleveland, which had been a largely stagnant town before the Ohio and Erie Canal, emerged as a hub shipping western commodities like wheat, corn and lumber to New York City and eastern manufactured goods to western markets. The canals were important because it was the first transportation technology to challenge the primacy of the Ohio River and the Appalachian Mountains, and it was the first transportation technology as well to chip away at this pan-Mississippian world.

Railroads continued what the canals began. The first railroads in Ohio were very often financed by British investment and it was the Baltimore and Ohio Railroad in the mid 1850s that was the first to cross the Appalachians into Ohio. By 1860, Ohio had built nearly three thousand miles of track, leading the nation. Railroad networks before the Civil War were about mostly in an east-west direction. That made New York more important to Ohio than New Orleans. Faster and cheaper travel improved profits and if the canals chipped away at the pan-Mississippian world then the railroads completely undermined it.

Leaving the pan-Mississippian world meant abandoning slavery. The problem for many white Ohioans was that both slavery and blacks threatened their growing sense of their state as a land of freedom, industry and morality. Black people, many whites believed, simply couldn't learn the individual skills and attain the required discipline to be economically independent. William Holmes McGuffey had taught Ohioans how to be sober, thrifty and hard-working but he hadn't taught them that those traits had nothing to do with race.

Ohioans rallied to the cause of anti-slavery only when, in the 1850s, southerners threatened Ohio as Ohioans had come to understand it. For example, in 1850 the US Congress passed the Fugitive Slave Law; this law created a group of federal commissioners who could issue warrants for the arrest of fugitives. A slave owner needed only testimony of a white witness or an affidavit from a slave state court to prove that the person was in fact a slave. The fugitive had no right to testify in his or her own behalf. The federal government also paid commissioners more when they ruled that the person in question was in fact a fugitive slave. Federal marshals were used to apprehend these fugitives and they could require citizens to offer their help. Refusing meant a fine and harboring a fugitive meant jail time. The Fugitive Slave Law of 1850 forced Ohioans to be directly complicit in slavery.

Slavery was no longer an economic transaction. Federal law required Ohioans, and all Americans, to help returned slaves to plantations. This law motivated Harriet Beecher Stowe to write Uncle Tom's Cabin. Stowe herself harbored fugitive slaves and other Ohioans openly disobeyed the Fugitive Slave Act. On September 13th, 1858, for example, a federal marshal in Oberlin, Ohio arrested a fugitive slave named John Price. To avoid conflict with local people, he took Price to nearby Wellington, Ohio. An Oberlin group then went to Wellington to free Price and the marshal, and his deputies took refuge in a local hotel. After peaceful negotiations failed, the mob stormed the hotel and found Price in the attic. They returned him to Oberlin where they hid him in the home of Oberlin College's president. A short time later, they took Price to freedom in Canada.

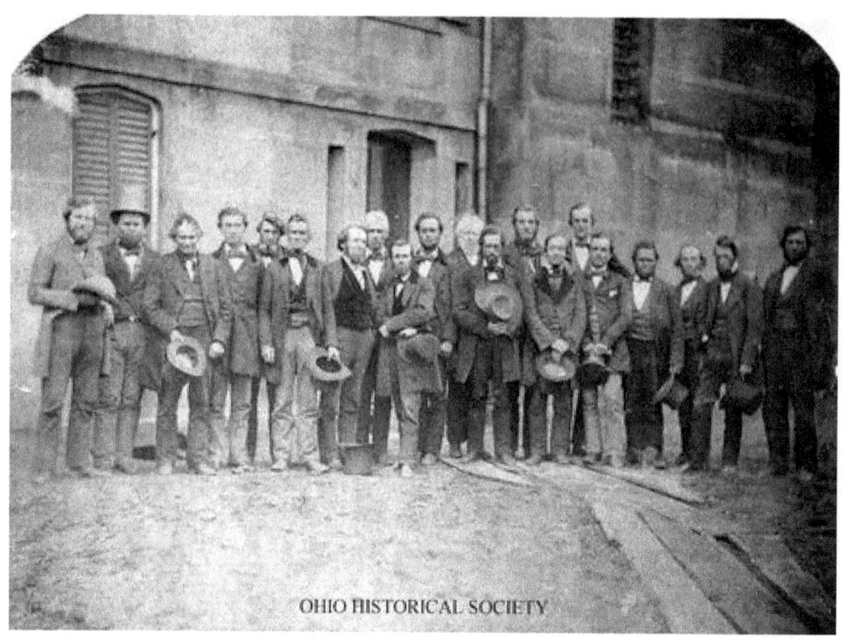

Men involved in the Oberlin-Wellington Rescue pose in front of the Cuyahoga County Jail, 1859.

A federal grand jury then indicted 37 of the people who freed Price. Ohio authorities responded by arresting the federal marshal, his deputies and other men involved. State and federal authorities cut a deal, charging only two men, one black and one white, with a crime. They were found guilty and sentenced to a short term. They appealed to the Ohio Supreme Court who upheld the constitutionality of the federal law. In response, more than 10,000 people participated in a Cleveland rally to oppose the Fugitive Slave Act.

We can see Ohio's break from the pan-Mississippian world in an editorial written by the Ohio State Journal in 1844. The journal said that a southerner was an "idle, pleasure seeking, heedless, improvident and extravagant" person who scarce moves hand or foot without the assistance of crouching abject slaves. That word "southerner" implies that no longer were Kentuckians, Alabamians and Mississippians considered westerners and united with Ohio. Instead, they were southerners and Ohioans were northerners.

When war came, Ohioans were intent on changing the south; reforming it and rebuilding it to make it look more like Ohio. Ohio provided some of the best leadership with the war on either side with Ohio born generals Ulysses Grant and William Tecumseh Sherman. By December 1st, 1864, nearly 350,000 Ohio soldiers were in service to the Union, the third most of any state behind only Pennsylvania and New York. A few thousand of them went to war knowing of, and perhaps even having participated in, the European revolutions of 1848. Those revolutions to throw off unrepresentative governments and extend democratic rights to more people.

This was possible because overall, there were 20 to 25 percent of the Union military forces that were foreign-born during the Civil War. In Ohio, there were approximately 20,000 German-born Ohio soldiers. These German immigrants created international networks and they exchanged information all the time. They heard, read and conversed about those revolutions and some of them even participated in them. When they failed, as many did, they left and immigrated to the US. For many German-born soldiers in Ohio, the US Civil War was a second chance to get the revolution right. We all know how the Civil War ended.

In northern Union county, there were many soldiers who volunteered to join the Ohio Volunteer Infantry (OVI) and the Ohio

Volunteer Calvary (OVC) regiments. Over 130 men from the Richwood area, probably more, died during the Civil War with much of them resting in unmarked and unnumbered graves. Some were killed in service or died of wounds and others by disease. A few soldiers in question I'd like to touch on; their personal lives and reminisces. It helps to not only bring a face to these soldiers but also describe what they went through during the bloodiest war in US history.

* * *

The first man I'd like to discuss is Samuel Adam McNeil. He was born in a log cabin on April 13, 1844 in York Township, Ohio. His father, Andrew McNeil, came to the township from Pennsylvania in the year 1839 and had since been a permanent resident except for four years where he resided in Marysville during his two terms of Office as Auditor of Union County in 1848. Andrew was also Commissioner of the county for six years. He was one of the most prominent men of Union County. Since the organization of the York Presbyterian Church, in 1839, he had been a Ruling Elder. Andrew was regarded as one of the early settlers of Union County.

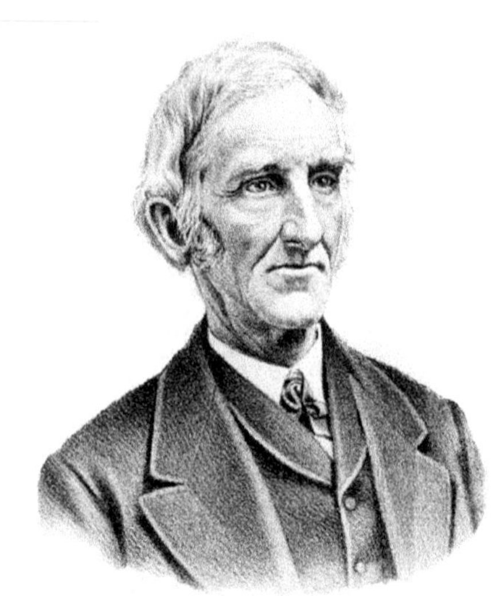

Portrait of Andrew McNeil during his time as Union County Auditor circa 1850.

Union County was, to a great degree, a frontier settlement during his boyhood years. Samuel McNeil acquired his education in the schools of the neighborhood and through the summer months, worked on his father's farm aiding in the development and cultivation of the homestead. He joined the York Presbyterian Church on March 26, 1858, when he was fourteen years old, thus early in life laying the foundation for a Reverent Christian career.

Early in 1861, his father arranged to send him away to school. But the dark cloud of the Civil War had gathered and loomed over the country, and young Samuel was determined to fight for the Union against the Confederate States. In June of 1861, when he was only seventeen years old, Samuel enlisted in the 13th Ohio Volunteer Infantry, but was released at the request of his father, on account of his youth and size. On August 17th, of the same year, he enlisted again, this time in Company F of the 31st Ohio Volunteer Infantry, for a term of three years.

They were detailed to do duty near Danville, Kentucky. Here, the 31st, 17th, and 88th Ohio and the 12th Kentucky were organized into the 4th Brigade and placed under the command of General George H. Thomas. The brigade was first under fire at Mill Springs on January 1st, 1862. Samuel took part in all of the campaigns of the Army of the Cumberland, including the battles of Stone River, Chickamauga, and the terrible assault at Mission Ridge, where he was very severely wounded on November 25, 1863.

The Battle of Missionary Ridge was fought on November 25th as part of the Chattanooga Campaign. More than 50,000 Union soldiers stormed the Confederate defenses along Missionary Ridge east of Chattanooga. The attack stretched from the Rossville Gap at the Georgia border all the way up to Tunnel Hill at the northern end of Missionary Ridge. By the end of the day, the Confederate Army of Tennessee was retreating towards Dalton, Georgia and Chattanooga was firmly in Union hands. It was, as one Confederate officer later described it, "The death knell of the Confederacy."

During this battle, Samuel was shot through the neck by a Minié ball, a type of bullet shot with a rifled musket; they were used extensively during the Civil War. He was conveyed to the hospital where he remained for about 30 days. All of his Company F, except eight, re-enlisted. He returned in January as a veteran and was promoted to Sergeant in time to take part in the Atlanta Campaign, and was with General William T. Sherman during General Joseph E. Johnston's surrender in April of 1865.

Samuel was 21 years of age the day that he was honorably discharged on July 26, 1865. At the close of the war, he went to work on his father's farm and remained at home until his marriage in 1866 to Martha E. Miller who was the youngest daughter of Mr. Chas Miller. He remained a resident of Union County until 1871 when he traveled with his family to live in Brown County, Kansas. He remained there for 7 years until he returned due to his parent's failing health. In 1881, Samuel's wife passed away after a failed birth with their fourth child. His infant son tarried long enough to make his presence felt and then was taken home, to welcome the mother, who in a few short years would follow him. Through untiring efforts, he held his family of little ones together and brought them to manhood and womanhood.

It wasn't until November 4, 1890 that Samuel remarried to Mrs. Hester Howland Ross, who had been his wife and companion for almost twenty-two years. On returning to his old home, he immediately united with the old church of his youth and took up the work there, which to those who knew him, knows was no small share. He was again called to leave his old home and assume larger duties, this time serving his native state in an official capacity in the old capitol building at Columbus. To this city he carried his master's work with him, uniting with the second, now known as the Central Presbyterian church, of Columbus, where he entered actively in the work. When his work there was accomplished he, with his wife, returned to Richwood where he united with the First Presbyterian Church. In 1897, he was elected as secretary and treasurer of the Regimental Reunion Association for life. He was also secretary of the Brigade Association and held many minor offices.

Samuel's death occurred due to suicide by hanging. His body was found in his office at the Richards Building on the corner of Franklin and Ottawa Streets which was just across the hall from the Richwood Telephone Company. According to the Richwood Gazette, his funeral was one of the most largely attended and most impressive to have ever been held in Richwood. It was held on his family residence on South Franklin Street on Monday afternoon at half past 2 on August 26th, 1912. A sketch of his life was read aloud by Reverend J.R. Lloyd, pastor of the First Presbyterian Church. Reverend Leon Arpee, a former pastor of the local church and intimate friend of Mr. McNeil, offered a few touching remarks. Commander George Montgomery of the Grand Army Post conducted the regular religious service of the organization. Tears flowed freely as the remnant of the old G.A.R. quartet, of which Sam McNeil himself was a member, sang "He Was My Comrade" and other familiar selections. The pall bearers were the elders of the First Presbyterian Church and veterans of the Grand Army Post and surviving members of Company F of the 31st Ohio Volunteer Infantry. His remains were taken to Claibourne Cemetery and placed in the mausoleum where it is still located to this day.

* * *

The second man I'd like to present is John Aller. Mr. Aller was born on December 3rd, 1843, near the village of Lockwin, Delaware County, Ohio. He did a good, thrifty job of growing his estate until the start of the war. John's heart prompted him to offer his services as a soldier. He made an effort to enlist in the 18th US Infantry but was rejected on account of his age. A short time after this, John took "French leave" from home and went to Urbana, where he succeeded in getting himself mustered in as a private in Company E of the 66th Regiment, OVI, on the 6th of January 1862. The regiment was soon ordered to West Virginia. The train on which they were being transported met with an accident which caused the death of several soldiers. Mr. Aller was injured to such an extent as to necessitate being sent to the hospital for a short time. He soon joined his company and served through its many bloody campaigns.

The 66th received its first taste of war at the Battle of Port Republic. This battle was fought on June 9, 1862 in Rockingham County, Virginia. During a stampede at this battle, John was knocked down and run over by a panic-stricken cavalryman and considerably injured. After extricating himself and recovering from the shock, he made an effort to find his company and, while so engaged, was captured by three Confederate Cavalrymen who started to march him off, but he soon found an opportunity to make an escape which he did not fail to make use of.

The next fight in which the 66th took a prominent role was the Battle of Cedar Mountain. The regiment was also present for the battles at Antietam, Chancellorsville, Gettysburg and Second Bull Run. The Battle of Gettysburg involved a large number of casualties and is sometimes described as the war's turning point. At

Gettysburg, Major General George Meade halted Robert E. Lee's army and stopped his invasion of the North. This was also where President Abraham Lincoln gave his famous Gettysburg Address by honoring the fallen Union soldiers.

The command of the 66th was then transferred to the Southwest, where it signified its presence by taking an active part in the Battle of Lookout Mountain on November 24, 1863. After this they made the Atlanta Campaign, doing their share of all the hard duties incident to that momentous movement. At the time of skirmishing and fighting around Kennasaw Mountain, Mr. Aller became sick and had to be sent to the convalescent camp at Chattanooga. As soon as he had made his recovery, he rejoined his Regiment at Goldsboro, North Carolina, on the same day that General Lee surrendered to General Grant.

John Aller was discharged at Louisville, Kentucky on the 15th of July 1865. John then returned to Union County, to the home of his parents, where he enjoyed all the honors which were bestowed on a returned soldier at the time. On March 27, 1867, Mr. Aller married Harriet Russel. They surrounded themselves with seven children. John and his family lived on a farm about two miles west of Richwood. He was a faithful member of Livingston Post, G.A.R., and held the place of Officer of the Guard. He died due to complications with pneumonia on December 24, 1926 at 83 years old. Three daughters survived at the time of his death along with 15 grandchildren and eight great-grandchildren.

* * *

Our third and final sketch is a little bit different from the rest. Washington Holmes was born a slave in Kentucky in 1852. His mother was sold to a slave dealer in the "Cotton States," before he was old enough to remember her. Washington never heard anything about her. They were not allowed to know anything about those matters and were punished if they were caught with a paper or book in their hands trying to read. As a result, Washington had very little education. He was able to read a little but learned since coming to Ohio. He had this to say about his children, "I want my children educated and am buying them books and clothes that they may attend school. Some teachers do not take as much pains with their recitations as they do with white children. Yes, there may be exceptions, but not many. I think it is best to have separate Colored Schools, where there are enough colored children to form them. Would want a colored teacher. It would make the scholars try harder to learn if they thought they might themselves become teachers."

When he was set at liberty and turned loose from the only home he had ever known, Washington did not know anything other than work; that was all they were allowed to know. Washington recalls how they treated them just as people do their horses; some masters treated their slaves kindly, and some did not. Some gave them an acre of ground to tend as their own, a pig to fatten, and dressed and led them well. While others would give them the roughest kind of food and dress them with nothing but the cheapest and poorest kind of clothing, usually the kind of clothes which barely hung on their bodies.

Washington's master owned around 150 to 200 slaves. He was as good to them as most masters were, "Oh yes, he worked us hard, but we didn't know anything else but to work. We sometimes ran away and went to town of an evening, but if we were caught without a pass from our master, we were arrested and lodged in jail until our owner came, and then punished." Washington's master, Archie Manmock, was in the rebel army, and was killed at Fort Fisher. Manmock's wife remained on the plantation where Mr. Holmes remained until 1868, when he was hired with Edward Hockiday for $12.00 a month. He worked for him for two years and then went to work as a section hand on the Baltimore & Ohio Railroad. He got $1.50 a day while working there.

Washington came to Ohio in 1872 and worked on a farm in Franklin county for about six years. He got married on Sept. 8, 1890, to Miss Eliza Davis. She had also been a slave; her master's name was Seymore McNeal. Seymore lived in West Virginia and had about 150 slaves. Eliza's father, Henry Davis, was his tea master and her mother, Amanda Davis, was his cook. She describes the man as being very cruel. Her mother had to cook for all the slaves, get separate meals for the master and mistress, knit so many "finger-lengths" each day, and weave so many yards of carpet after supper. At the breaking out of the war, Eliza's father, along with 17 other slaves, carried out a daring plot to escape to Ohio. Without knowing in which direction to go, the Union soldiers helped them off, got them on a train and told them where to change cars. After the war, he came back after his wife and the children. Eliza's mother was still living near Columbus, about 80 years old, by the time Eliza and Washington got married.

Mr. and Mrs. Holmes removed to Washington township, Union County in April 1889. They had a family of five children and strived hard to have them educated. Their family moved to Marion, Ohio a couple years later until Washington passed away due to liver cancer on March 31, 1908. Eliza remarried to Plez Claybourne on September 28, 1919. She was a member of the Bethel M.E. Church where her funeral services were conducted after passing away on December 6, 1938 at the age of about 85. She is currently buried in the Historic Marion Cemetery along with Washington and Plez. Records indicate that all three were buried without headstones.

Chapter 6

EARLY 1900S

Ohio became a creative and dynamic place circa 1900 and the state was at its peak around this time. From 1868 to 1920, Ohio won the presidential election nine out of 14 times. World-changing technology was also invented in Ohio in this period including the airplane and the electric ignition system for automobiles. Ohioans led the world in attempts to make the world a better place for working-class families for the people who went down in the mineshaft and who worked the furnace at the steel mill; in other words, the people who did the dirty and dangerous work of building modern America. The union movement was important to Ohio as many important unions were founded in Columbus such as the American Federation of Labor in 1886 and the United Mine Workers in 1890.

The Prohibition Movement, a movement to compel people to stop drinking, was also started in Ohio. It was led by the Anti-Saloon League which was founded in Oberlin, Ohio in 1893 and relocated to Westerville, a suburb of Columbus, in 1909. This movement was led mostly by men and they focused their efforts on the abolition of the sale of alcohol through outlets such as saloons. They named their organization the Anti-Saloon League in order to tell the American public that they opposed the political power of immigrants. Often in large cities, the saloon was the politician's office; it became a power base in immigrant neighborhoods. The Anti-Saloon League was effective and influential, more than any other organization. They helped persuade America to amend the Constitution, ratifying the 18th amendment in 1919 to outlaw the manufacture and distribution of alcohol.

Cleveland ranked 5th in the world in terms of the importance of its inventions to the industrial world. These inventions ranged from oil refining techniques, to processes to unload iron ore from ships, to the electric railway. There was also the Cleveland-based Winton Motor Company, the first US company to sell an automobile and in 1900, the largest producer of gasoline-powered cars. Then there was Dayton which, in 1900, the city had more scientific patents per capita than any other US city at the time. The Dayton Engineering Laboratories Company, or Delco, invented the electrical ignition system for cars.

Richwood was no stranger to inventions either. In 1886, Harry E. Owen built one of the very first automobiles not just in Richwood but in America. He was employed as an auto designer by Packard, Maxwell Auto, Wener Gear and Chrysler. It was said that he designed and built an automobile at the age of 14. The first thing Owen decided he needed was a foundry, but he couldn't afford a large one since his finances consisted of only $12. Of this money, $2.50 was spent on a crucible pot, which he used to melt brass given to him by his friends who were employees of the Erie railroad. His father, Dr. T.C. Owen, was a surgeon for the railroad. Melted brass didn't mean much without patterns, so the youth haunted the stores getting pine boxes until finally the patterns were made. These were modeled with a pocketknife and the use of his father's surgical instruments.

He was able to travel to Marion to obtain sand for his molds. Several men with whom he was acquainted in a foundry at Marion gave him a bushel of sand. Next he went to a blacksmith shop in Richwood to use a forge for his work. It was here that lack of knowledge nearly drowned the enthusiasm of the young inventor. He couldn't temper the sand to suit him, and experienced trouble getting the proper vents and anchoring cores. Finally, he succeeded in getting the casing which would fit his needs. Owen solicited the aid of the owners of a Richwood machine shop to finish the parts before assembly. His wheels were iron cultivator wheels with axles and springs from a buggy. After many weeks of work, he finally assembled the automobile in 1886. Not much else is known about the automobile or what happened to it. Owen went on to build an auto for Thomas Manufacturing in Springfield in 1899. In 1901, he designed another for Trumble Manufacturing in Warren, Ohio. The man held patents for three of his inventions; a patent on light shading devices was received on June 20, 1922, and on April 15, 1924, a patent on utility receptacles and armrests for automobiles was granted. The man died on July 7, 1938 in Springfield at the age of 64 after suffering a cerebral hemorrhage.

Another man by the name of John A. Scharf incorporated a company that manufactured automobiles in Richwood on November 27, 1912. The president of the company became George W. Worden, the publisher of the Richwood Gazette at the time. Scharf served on the board of directors and also held a patent of a device from which the company was founded. This device was developed in Scharf's machine shop, the building of which later became Web Plastics on North Fulton Street. The Scharf Gearless Motor Car Company, as it was called, built a demonstration auto which remained in possession of Scharf's daughter, Loretta Brown, until about 1967. This automobile was then sold to a private collector. The car was driven by a small wheel that turned a large disc mounted on the rear axle. The small wheel, which was connected to the engine by a sliding shaft and operating on the side of the large disc, was moved closer to the edge of the disc for more power and closer to the axle for more speed. This function was apparently controlled by a centrifugal governor and thus in effect became the first automatic transmission. This principle is still used today in some power motors.

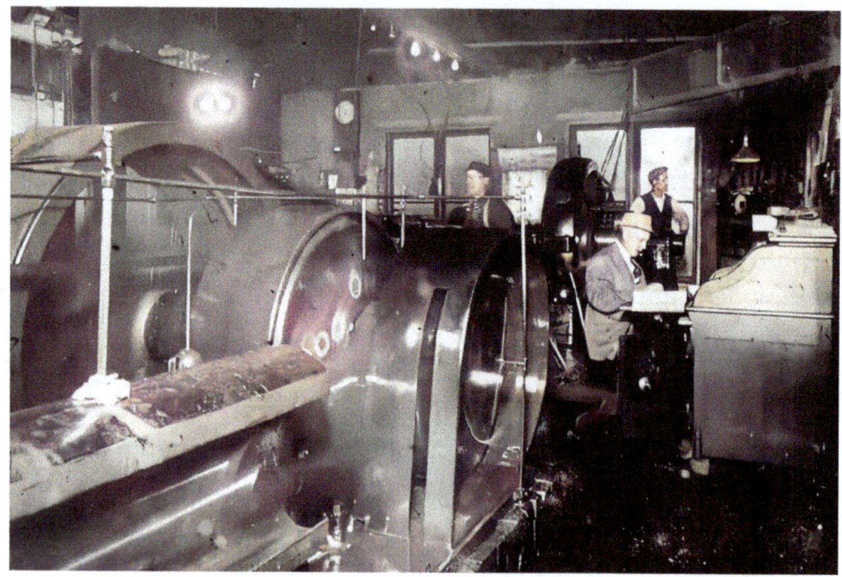

The generator at the Richwood Power and Light Co. It furnished early electricity to the people of Richwood. Photo taken circa 1900 (colorized).

Electricity came to Richwood on Thursday, October 13, 1898. Edward A. Schambs built a light plant, called the Richwood Power and Light Co., in a brick building on the west side of North Franklin Street. He installed a 200-horsepower steam boiler and engine, a sixty-light arc light dynamo and a 500-light dynamo for incandescent lights. This latter contraption was a direct current dynamo-modern power lines carry alternating current. The voltage was 110 which is approximately similar to modern usage. Mr. Schambs hoped to start up during the Richwood Fair, but delays occurred forcing him to open ten days later. Crews set poles and strung wire downtown and arc lights were installed. Mayor M.W. Hill turned the lights on for the first time. He was heard saying "Let there be light," as he inserted a plug switch and the lights switched on, illuminating the village. The company grew in size and importance until 1918 when the light plant ceased generating its power locally and bought from the Columbus, Delaware & Marion Electric Company plant, which began to furnish power to both the local interurban railway along with the village of Richwood. The power in the village was eventually taken over by Ohio Edison owned by First Energy Corp.

The first radio was also built in Richwood, by accident no less, on March 4, 1922 by J.H. Sanders, Vernal Zuspan, and David Haines. The men were experimenting with a telephone receiver and were startled to hear voices out of thin air. They had tuned into an experimental broadcast from New Jersey. The next day, they built a more efficient device and obtained their needed parts from the Richwood Light Company plant. They succeeded and managed to hear broadcasts from Cleveland and Detroit. Other people around Richwood built radio receivers shortly thereafter. Edward A. Schambs built a receiver for the light plant with an added amplifier and loudspeaker. Those who visited the office of the light company were able to hear the broadcasts received.

World War I, fought from 1914 the 1918, introduced many hardships in Richwood. Fuel was in short supply during the winter of 1916-1917. Coal started to be used more predominantly instead of wood which required transportation by train. The US didn't enter the conflict until 1917 as we had been engaged in the Mexican Border War from 1910 to 1919. Farmers did what they could to plant as much as possible in their fields. Those living in town were urged to plant large gardens and save as much produce as possible. Tin became a war material so canned goods became expensive and rare. The coal shortage worsened by the end of 1917. It was reported that around 250 families in Richwood were without fuel. The local high school was forced to close, and the light plant was forced to cease operations a few times.

During this time, Richwood was officially "dry", but whiskey was still considered a medicine and was available for purchase at drug stores. Wheat flour was restricted, and people were forced to use substitutes like rice flour, corn meal and barley. Children saved rags to make paper for the war effort and had scrap drives, the metal for which was used to make guns. Peach pits were donated to be used for cyanide and grease which was used to make nitroglycerin. The first soldier from Richwood to die in the war was Carl Fausnaugh. He died on December 26 in France due to pneumonia.

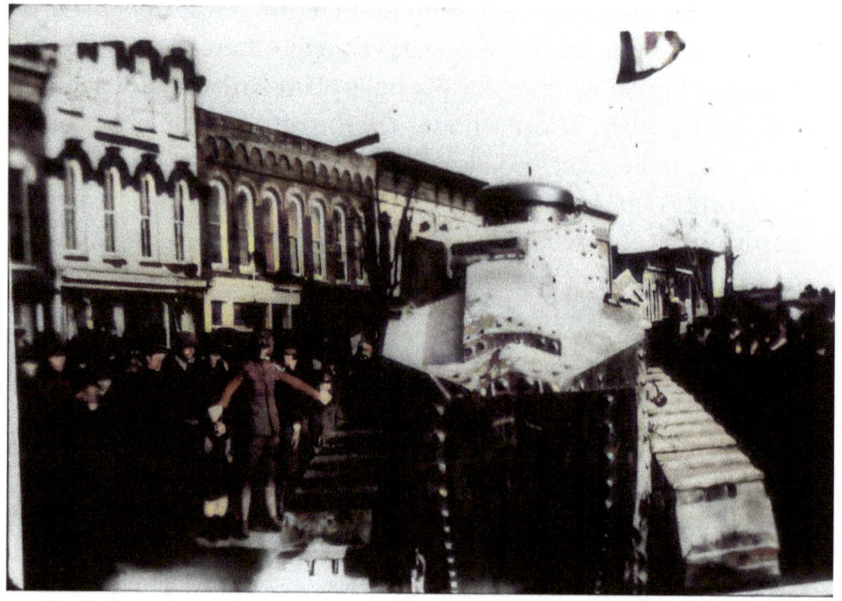

An M1917 tank was shown off to the citizens of Richwood after the war on April 22, 1919 (colorized).

After World War I, immigration turned into a perceived negative. Strangers seemed to bring more danger than value. This shift was about conflict between working-class Americans and wealthy factory owners. In 1919, across the nation, but especially in Ohio, waves of strikes hit industrial towns. In Ohio alone there were 237 strikes and while the strikes involved several industries, the steel industry was the hardest hit; 100,000 Ohio steel workers went on strike. All of these strikes were local in scope, a fight between specific workers and owners in a factory town over wage cuts and increased hours. The owners of factories explained that these strikes were part of a conspiracy planned by foreigners. The owners reminded native-born Ohioans that most of their factory workers were foreign-born and thus a bit suspicious. Cultural norms in Ohio started to openly question whether immigrants had the discipline and the character to be good Americans. How could they be if they were always in saloons?

The context of the Russian Revolution aided the owners and their attempts to smear the workers. In 1917, the Bolsheviks led by Vladimir Lenin overthrew the Russian government and instituted a communist regime. The factory owners successfully frightened middle-class people, persuading them that the immigrants who lived across town were taking their cues from Lenin and that they were intent on abolishing private property and overthrowing the American government. And it worked.

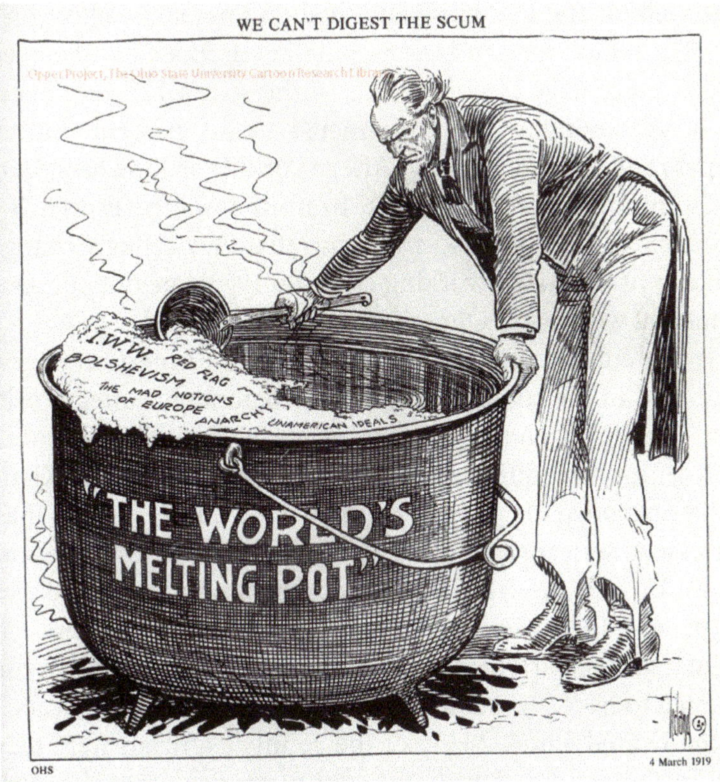

Editorial from the Columbus Dispatch, March 1919. Uncle Sam is scooping out the "scum" from "The World's Melting Pot."

Ever since Cincinnati exploded the preeminent status on the frontier, tensions over immigration hadn't been a defining part of life in Ohio. But by 1920, the forces of xenophobia had gained national power. In a federal government that was far more capable than it had been in 1850, it now had the bureaucratic expertise, the finances, and the law enforcement resources to severely restrict immigration. In 1921, President Warren G. Harding, a republican from Ohio, signed into law a quota system that made it more difficult for immigrants from Southern and Eastern Europe to enter the country. It would be the first in a series of anti-immigrant steps in the 1920s that greatly favored Northern Europeans and immigrants from the Western Hemisphere over Italians, Russians and eastern and central Europeans.

Harding and his Republicans passed these laws in part because immigrants from Southern and Eastern Europe were more likely to vote Democratic and these laws had an immediate effect on Ohio. By 1930, Ohio's foreign-born population dropped by 10 percent, the lowest percentage of immigrants in the state's 127-year history. In 1910, that number had plummeted to 4.1 percent. But factory owners still needed workers. After World War I, owners set out on an ambitious plan to recruit from the south, especially from Appalachia. They were so ambitious that they actually changed the makeup of the state's working class. By 1973, one out of every three industrial workers in Ohio were from Appalachia.

In the context of the rapid rise of African American migrants to Ohio and in the context of increased xenophobia after World War I, the Ku Klux Klan rose to prominence in Ohio. The Klan of the late 19th century was different than the one in the 1920s. The Klan of the 1920s extended its prejudice to include more groups than just African Americans and extended its reach to beyond the southern states. In fact, the KKK was especially strong in Ohio during the 1910s and 1920s. For example, by 1923 and 1924 there were an estimated 400,000 Ohioans in the Klan. In Summit County, the Klan claimed to have 50,000 members making it the largest local chapter in the United States. Many of the county's officials were members too including the sheriff, the Akron mayor, several judges and County Commissioners and most members of the Akron school board. The Klan used bigoted laws and violence to compel Ohio to look the way they thought it should.

An article in the Richwood Gazette notes that a KKK meeting was held on October 4, 1923 in Magnetic Springs. It was estimated that around 3,000 people attended the meeting. The Gazette states that, "Several good talks were given, and an excellent quartet sang to the crowd's delight." Meetings were also held in Richwood as well. The Women of the Ku Klux Klan had a meeting on September 21, 1923 held in the Maccabees hall which was located over Zebold's Millinery Store in the Hastings Building. All women of the vicinity were invited. The notice describes that a state speaker was in attendance and presented a speech for the cause.

An event also occurred in Plain City on February 3, 1923. Saturday night at the hour of nine, a burning cross was seen on a vacant lot opposite the schoolhouse on the main street of the village. Thirty minutes later, residents were startled to see 32 men, by actual count, garbed in white hoods and robes, march up Main Street from the direction of the road to Columbus. These men carried banners on which were inscribed "Law and Order Bootleggers Beware," "White Supremacy," and "Christian Religion."

Silently, the masked figures approached the fiery cross, about-faced, and retraced their steps to the outskirts of the village where a score of autos waited. Not a word was uttered, nor was there a sound, except for the clapping of hands by a number of strangers, unmasked, who came into the village earlier in the evening. Citizens stared at each other and speculated. Mayor J.B. Parker regarded the incident lightly. He exclaimed that, "They didn't do anything but march up the 'main drag,' burn their cross, and depart." But it was an event that upset the city nonetheless.

Chapter 7

THE GREAT DEPRESSION

Due to being one of the leading industrial economies in the country, Ohio was hard hit by the global depression of the 1930s. In 1930, unemployment reached 13.3% of Ohio's population and by 1932, that number had skyrocketed to 37.3%. In Toledo, unemployment at its height hit 80% of the city's population. Even if you're lucky enough to have a job, your paycheck in Ohio on average declined from 33% from 1929 to 1932. Ohio farmers struggled as well as the price per bushel of wheat dropped from a high of 94 cents in 1914 to 40 cents by 1933. The Depression also made worse an already difficult agricultural market. From 1925 to 1935, 20% of all Ohio farms changed ownership because of economic difficulties.

African Americans felt the effects of the Depression first and longest because they were often relegated to marginal jobs and were the last hired and first fired. In a 1930 survey, 90% of Cincinnati employers said either that they did not want to hire African Americans, or they refused to answer the question at all. No wonder then that by 1933, unemployment within Cincinnati's African American population was 54% and even though African Americans comprise only 10% of the city's population, they made up 25% of the city's unemployment rate. So overall, the statistical picture was grim as Ohio suffered immensely in the Great Depression. By 1938, there were more Ohioans receiving federal systems than residents of any other state except Pennsylvania. Ohio also led the nation in two categories no state ever wants to lead in, job loss and decline in industrial output.

The Democrats, led by Franklin Delano Roosevelt, concluded that an unequal distribution of income was the root of the problem. In the 1920s, the share of income increased for the wealthiest Americans but decreased for most everybody else. For example, in 1920 the richest 1% controlled 12% of the national income. In 1929, however, they controlled 19%. Also, by 1929, the richest 10% of Americans controlled 40% of the nation's disposable income. In other words, wealth was increasingly centralized in the hands of fewer and fewer wealthy families. As a consequence, mass purchasing power was tapped out. By 1929, with wages stretched thin and credit lines maxed out, fewer refrigerators and automobiles could be bought. This fundamental weakness exposed all sorts of other imbalances in the economy, and it triggered the Depression.

Within Ohio, the business and political elite tended to rely on traditional ideas. Poverty and unemployment, for example, suggested an individual character flaw. You were poor or unemployed because of something you did or failed to do; you didn't work hard enough, and you spent your money unwisely or you simply hadn't improved your skills to remain in demand as a worker. As a result, whatever relief we the community offered to you in your time of need should be local because we know your flaws best and can watch how you spend or misspend our charity. It should be private because public tax dollars shouldn't be involved in charity and it should be insufficient because we don't want to subsidize your character flaws. In general, whatever reason you lost your job, you should just wait out the downturn. Struggle is good for you; hardship provides moral depth to success.

But not everybody defined the Depression in such terms. President Franklin Roosevelt and his supporters sought to redress persistent and destructive inequalities of wealth. They chose not to blame individuals for the misery caused by an economic system that had exploited them and then tossed them aside when convenient. They chose to do that not by using federal power to redistribute wealth, in other words, they didn't simply jack the tax rate up on millionaires and pass them around to the poor, nor did they take control of private businesses and banks. FDR and the new dealers instead used the federal government to empower people. In particular, they sought to protect and encourage an individual's ability to create a better life, to make their families more economically secure and they did this in a variety of ways. Most importantly, they supported Unions.

In 1935, Congress passed, and FDR signed into law, the Wagner Act which legitimized the basic right of workers to unionize and to choose on their own their union and their leaders and to collectively bargain with employers. FDR's goal was not to create a soviet-style worker collective. Rather, it was to even the playing field between workers and owners; to give workers a chance to negotiate higher wages, better benefits and safer working environments. The workers themselves could negotiate a healthier and wealthier life. That alone could not equalize the disparities between the richest and the poorest, but it would create better consumers. People who could sustain a dynamic mass-production economy.

Business and political elites, and certainly many voters as well, opposed the Wagner Act because unions, in their opinion, threatened the process by which people became good citizens. Individuals should work hard and persevere despite obstacles and delay purchases of luxuries by scrimping and saving, barely surviving until the economy turns for the better. Government welfare, jobs and protection of workers spoil the character of Ohioans. The key problem of the depression was really more about relying on individual moral standards and not reforming an economic system.

Of course, Ohio's workers disagreed. They said that improvement came only when people gathered together to fight established authorities and that pursuing self-interest would improve Ohio and make them better consumers. It will also put people back to work and will make the factory owners more profit. Workers believed that they should reform structural economic problems rather than obsess about individual morality. Ohio workers were leaders in the National Union movement. For example, the sit-down strike era began in Akron in 1934 when 1,100 workers struck the General Tire Company. A sit-down strike is a form of civil disobedience in which workers at their workstation stop the assembly line and sit down, occupying the factory. This tactic hindered police efforts to violently break a strike because the expensive machinery might get damaged. It also undermined the owners' ability to bring in workers to break the strike. The Akron workers successfully won better wages and working conditions. Their success also provided a model for a wave of sit-down strikes from 1936 to 1937. Ohioans joined that wave as approximately 250,000 Ohioans ranging across several mass production industries like the auto, steel and rubber industries went on strike using the Wagner Act as legal justification.

Another way that FDR and the New Deal helped secure a better future was the Works Progress Administration (WPA). The agency provided employment to millions of workers to carry out public works projects. It improved 20 airports across the state including an airport at Cleveland, employing around 4,000 workers. Dayton's very first airport was also constructed as a result of this agency. The Richwood water and sewer systems were installed as WPA projects as well as the construction of the second floor of the Opera House. The condition of rural roads in Ohio made livestock transportation difficult. The WPA began an extensive farm to market road program in which they converted old roads into excellent graded highways. Almost 4,500 miles of road and highway improvements and 5,000 blocks of city streets were included in this program.

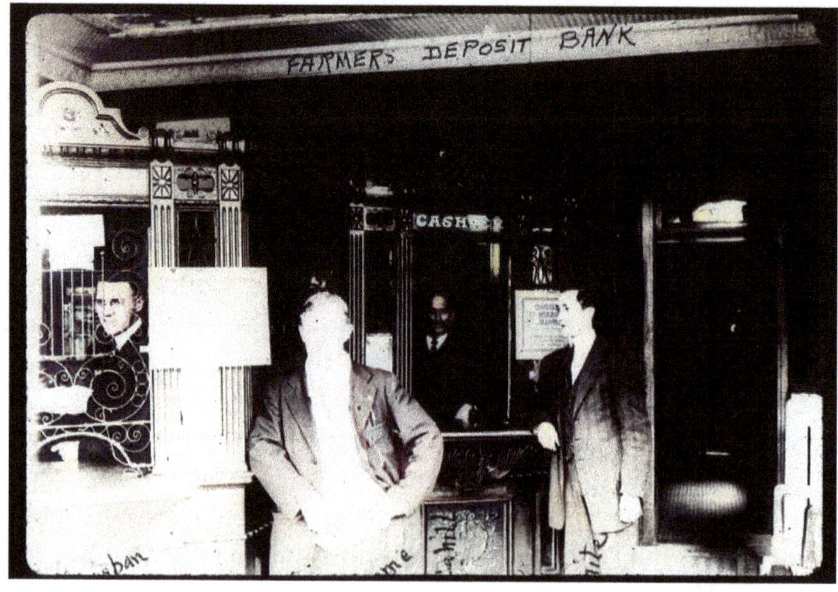

Farmers Deposit Bank was one of the two banks that closed in Richwood during the Depression. Photo taken circa 1920 (colorized).

Before the time of the Depression, most farmers had their own corn ground into meal for use in a variety of dishes. Some also had wheat ground into flour. The trouble with wheat, however, was that it had to be ground very fine and sifted through cloth in order to produce good flour. The flour mill burned down in Richwood a few years prior, and flour was hard to come by during these hard years. Many farmers grew an acre or two of sorghum cane to produce syrup, but this practice had mostly ceased before the second World War. The syrup was strong-tasting and not very palatable. Homemade butter was sold for ten cents a pound and eggs for ten cents a dozen in the years before the war.

During the Depression, entertainment was rare. Richwood decided to hold a street dance in the village to encourage local citizens and farmers to visit. The first dance was held on Halloween in 1930. Harry Cooper and his band, from Pharisburg, played as people partook in square dancing. Other dances weren't held until the summer of 1931. After this, the dances became a regular Saturday event. The dances were started by the businesses of Richwood as a way to lift spirits during the Depression. The dances were financed through the businesses as weekly donations. Lee Adams was in charge of getting the dances ready and did most of the financial collecting.

Franklin Street was coated with a substance that made the surface slippery enough to dance on. At first, a compound was used that was too slippery, so soap flakes were used instead. Musicians were housed in a shack made from a farm wagon which was enclosed on three sides and on top. Lee Adams setup the microphone and amplifier system since he was an electrician. Roller skaters also occupied the street, making the music do double duty. The dances were discontinued in 1937 when they were replaced with street carnivals.

The federal government furnished work, not just for laborers but artists and teachers as well. Adult classes were offered in Richwood by the WPA in 1937. A.P. Russell, county superintendent of schools and chairman of WPA Education, announced that classes could be taken on several subjects. All classes were free and open to everyone 16 and older. Rolland Dixon taught a music course in stringed instruments. Pearl Evans taught courses in home economics, rug and basket weaving, and bible study at her home.

The Civil Works Administration (CWA) was a predecessor of the WPA agency. It was a program that rapidly created hard labor jobs for those without work. By 1933, the CWA had 15 jobs in Union County which employed around 595 men out of 625 who held work cards which entitled them to work on federal projects. Participates of the program were limited to 30 hours a week. Workers earned around 50 cents an hour with skilled labor earning slightly more. CWA was involved in three projects in Richwood. Bethlehem and Claibourne Roads were improved, and tile was installed in the western part of town to improve drainage. It wasn't until World War II that Ohio and the rest of the country would start to improve.

Chapter 8

WORLD WAR II

The Second World War was fought from 1939 to 1945. The United States didn't publicly get involved in the beginning, although they were furnishing weapons and supplies to the Allies. The victories of Nazi Germany against Poland, Belgium, the Netherlands, and France, brought about increased urgency to the Roosevelt administration. They were discreetly preparing for possible involvement. On December 7, 1941, Japanese forces attacked Pearl Harbor in Hawaii. Japanese ambassadors were meeting at the State Department at the same time as the attack to discuss trade agreements. Many people were angered by this deception and the reaction by our government was immediate. Recruiting stations across the US were bombarded by people wanting to enlist. President Roosevelt spoke to Congress the next day and asked for a declaration of war.

The mayor of Richwood, Charles H. Brown, called for voluntary registration on January 22, 1942 of every person who could help in the defense of the village if it's ever necessary. Residents of Richwood were asked to register in the Council Room. Those able to drive trucks or cars, doctors and nurses, businessmen, schoolteachers, ministers, fire wardens and anyone who could help any way possible were sought after. Several citizens spent a lot of time in getting committees appointed and correspondences and other duties established.

Union County farmers did their share in the increased Food-for-Defense program. Approximately 70 percent of the cropland of the county was included in the increased farm production for 1942. Milk production was increased by 18 percent and cows from 10 to 12 percent in 1942 over 1941. Egg production increased 32 percent; hogs, 35 percent; beef cattle and veal calves 13 percent; soybeans, 30 percent; garden acreage 5 to 10 percent, with decreases in wheat and corn acreage.

Defense bonds were a way to finance the war effort. Roosevelt's advisors favored a system of tax increases influenced by British economist John Maynard Keynes. Keynes had just published his monograph, *How to Pay for the War*, where he suggested a way for wartime governments to institute tax increases and enforce a savings program. These steps increased spending while avoiding the risk of inflation. The defense bond program was implemented at the start of the war. They were sold for as little as $18.75 and matured in ten years in which time the government would pay the bondholder $25. 10 and 25 cent stamps were also available for purchase for those who found it difficult to afford an entire bond. When enough stamps were accumulated, the recipient could use them to purchase a bond.

On February 5, a sugar shortage was announced along with plans for rationing. During the first World War, sugar became scarce, sales were limited, and prices rose to exorbitant levels as high as thirty and forty cents per pound. But when the war ended, American warehouses were found to be bulging with hundreds of thousands of tons of sugar that could have been used during the war emergency. Sugar consumption in the United States during 1941 was approximately seven million tons, with about one million tons coming from the Philippines, which supply had been cut off. There was a Cuba sugar surplus of approximately one million two hundred thousand tons available for American use.

Under the New Deal agricultural policy, production of American sugar had been greatly restricted. In the beet sugar areas of Ohio, Michigan, Indiana and the far west, planting was so limited by government order that many sugar refineries were forced to close.

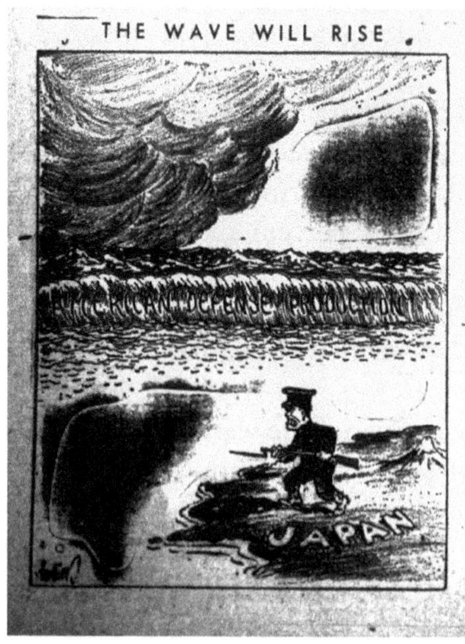

Political cartoon appearing in the Richwood Gazette circa 1942.

While restrictions on sugar production within continental United States were lifted in 1942, the crops had to first be planted, harvested and refined before the home-produced sugar could reach American tables. Sugar production in Cuba, Mexico, Central and South America, was also increased. It is claimed that the sugar shortage resulted from the need to use sugar for the manufacture of alcohol for war purposes. However, alcohol of exactly the same chemical content and nature can be made from corn, wheat and other grains, of which there were great surpluses, at a cost comparable to that of alcohol from sugar.

Around this time, books were also being requested for soldiers to read. The American Library Association advocated for the Victory Book Campaign which was sponsored by the ALA, American Red Cross and United Service Organizations. Although the Government had provided library buildings and trained librarians for Army Camps containing more than 5,000 men, their supply of books was not sufficient for the tremendous growth in the armed forces. Each company or battalion had a dayroom where books for an hour of rest were eagerly used. Just outside the camps were USO houses for men on leave, each of which contained a reading room with empty shelves.

Paul A. T. Noon, Ohio director of the Victory Book Campaign, said that good books of many kinds were needed—fiction, with the emphasis on adventure, well written, up-to date novels, mystery stories, humor and historical novels; recent technical books, especially aviation and radio; current affairs, government; history and biography, particularly in dramatic style; poems, plays, essays; and timely reference works. In short, exactly the books most of us like to own and read ourselves. Because of the difficulties in handling them, magazines were not desired. Heading the local campaign in Richwood was Mrs. Stanley Peet, who was assisted by the following committee members: Dr. H. C. Duke, chairman of publicity; Mrs. Richard Langstaff, Mrs. L. J. McCoy, Mrs. D. K. Davis, Mrs. Thad Sieg, Mrs. Perry Allen and Miss Lucille Smith. Books were to be taken to the Richwood Public Library. Anyone not able to bring in books were to contact Mrs. Peet and a Girl Scout would be sent for them.

Victory in Europe (VE Day) was announced by President Harry S. Truman over the radio at 9 a.m. on May 8, 1945. He called for a day of quiet rejoicing and prayer for the fight which continued to rage on in the Pacific. The "brownout" that was declared nationwide to save electricity for the war effort was ended. It was now legal again to light outdoor advertising and display windows and decorative lighting. The mayor of Richwood, C.H. Brown, ordered the fire siren sounded and asked local businesses to close for the day. Church services and home prayer were the order of the day.

The Victory over Japan (VJ Day) was later announced on August 14, 1945. This victory came after the first atomic bombs were dropped over Hiroshima and Nagasaki, Japan. The news was received in Richwood about 7 p.m. Five minutes afterward, uptown Richwood was crowded with automobiles with shrieking horns, church bells, guns and the old fire bell which was put into use once more after much persuasion. The fire siren shrieked for about a half hour. A steady downpour of rain didn't discourage people from celebrating. All stores were closed for the day due to the holiday announced by President Truman. After the demonstration, many citizens of Richwood went to Marion and Columbus to take part in the parades there.

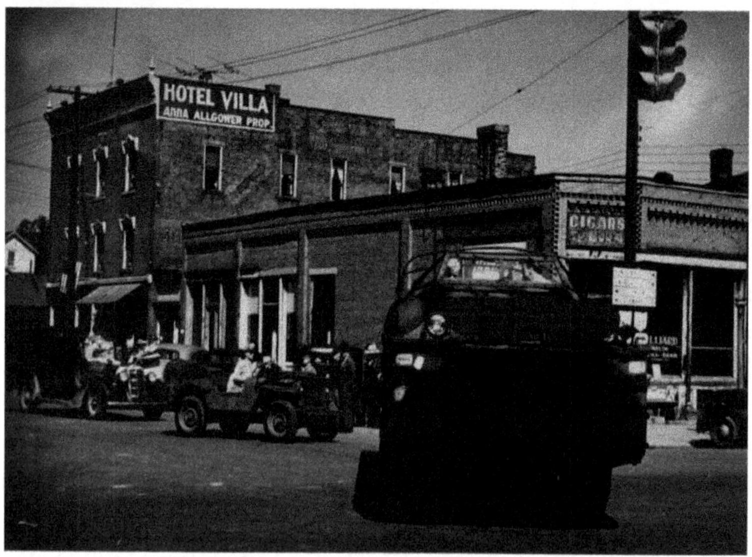

A parade in Richwood that occurred one year after the war on Memorial day in 1946 (colorized).

On Thursday evening, the Lions Club sponsored a dance in celebration of the victory. Richwood was the only town in central Ohio that sponsored a planned program and dance celebration of the Japanese surrender. The program was opened by Aaron Durnell singing "America," the entire crowd joining in with him. Mayor C.H. Brown gave a speech followed by Ruth Shuman singing "God Bless America"; talks were then given by Rev. Edward Brewster followed by prayer by Rev. C.E. Combrink. Jeanne Winter Harger and Helen Sullivan played several selections on their accordions. Sgt. Harry B. Sunday, who recently returned from 28 months service overseas with the 363rd Engineer Regiment Special Service Unit in Iran, gave a short talk on his experiences which was well received by the crowd. Miller's orchestra, from Pharisburg, played from 10 p.m. until 1 a.m. for a very large crowd.

Various stories were printed in the Richwood Gazette of those unaccounted for after the war and what may or may not have resulted in their untimely deaths. One example is Captain L. Chandler Baldwin, grandson of Frank L. Baldwin of Richwood and nephew of County Superintendent of Schools, Gale W. Baldwin.

Captain Baldwin was born in Tokyo while his father was serving as Military Attaché to the American Embassy there. He graduated from West Point in 1938 and had served at Corregidor Island for three years before the war with Japan. He was taken prisoner at the fall of Corregidor and was held in the Philippines until December of 1944 when he was put aboard a Japanese prison boat which carried 1,600 prisoners to Japan in order to prevent their rescue by American forces. When the unmarked prison boat was bombed by American planes, nearly 3/4ths of those on board were lost. Nothing had been heard of Captain Baldwin since that time. It was thought that he was taken to Japan and kept there until his death which resulted from brutalities and malnutrition.

Chapter 9

OPERA HOUSE

The Richwood Town Hall (later renamed the Opera House in the early 20th century) replaced the engine house in 1890. The first mention of a town hall in Richwood was on February 28, 1889 in the Richwood Gazette. An effort was to be made to give Richwood a much-needed town hall large enough to hold a few hundred people. The plan was to build the hall via taxation.

An article in the Richwood Gazette on March 28, 1889 furthered the demand for a town hall. They interviewed various citizens of Richwood; most all of them strongly favored a town hall to be built provided it wouldn't cost the town too much. A man named George Gum went to a large number of citizens and talked to them about levying a tax to build a hall. He had this to say: "I talked to businessmen about this thing till I was tired. They all wanted a hall, but nothing was done, and I let the matter drop. I understand a party wants the old engine house, and if the town can sell that it ought to do it. A new jail is needed and will probably have to be built right away. My idea is to put up a good building, with a jail, mayor's office, township office, engine room, ect., on the first floor and a town hall on the second. And while we're about it, we ought to put a good building. It ought to be done by taxation, but I would give twenty-five dollars in addition to my share of the taxes to get the thing started." It was later this week when the Ohio Legislature was asked to give the citizens of Richwood a chance to vote on the question of building a town hall. Many signatures were obtained.

Senator Cutler introduced Senate Bill 599 to authorize the council of the Village of Richwood to issue bonds for the purpose of purchasing grounds and building a town hall with a fire department, corporation offices and other purposes. The bill successfully passed both houses and became law on April 2, 1889. A section of the bill reads as follows: "Section 1. Be it enacted by the General Assembly of the State of Ohio, That the village council of the village of Richwood, Union county, be and is hereby authorized to borrow money and issue bonds therefor, not to exceed ten thousand dollars, for the purpose of purchasing suitable grounds, and build thereon a town hall, fire department buildings, corporation offices, and jail; said bond to be of such denominations as said council may deem best, and shall run for a period not to exceed six per cent, per annum, interest to be paid semi-annually, and to be sold for not less than their par value."

After the Village Council passed the resolution, the election was held on May 25, 1889. The resolution passed 145 to 54 in favor of a town hall. Only 199 votes were cast in regard to the bill. It was presumed that those who didn't vote didn't strongly oppose the building or else they would've gone to the polls. The building was expected to cost less than $10,000.

However, the cost ended up being a lot more than originally thought. While the Council decided that the building cost no more than $8,000, the talk with some contractors put the cost to more than $15,000. This created somewhat of a panic within the community and a town meeting was held to discuss the recent changes. A few citizens expressed opposition to the building based solely on the alleged heavy cost. The village council agreed that the architect's estimates were too high, and a resolution was passed to wait a while longer so that they can explore other solutions.

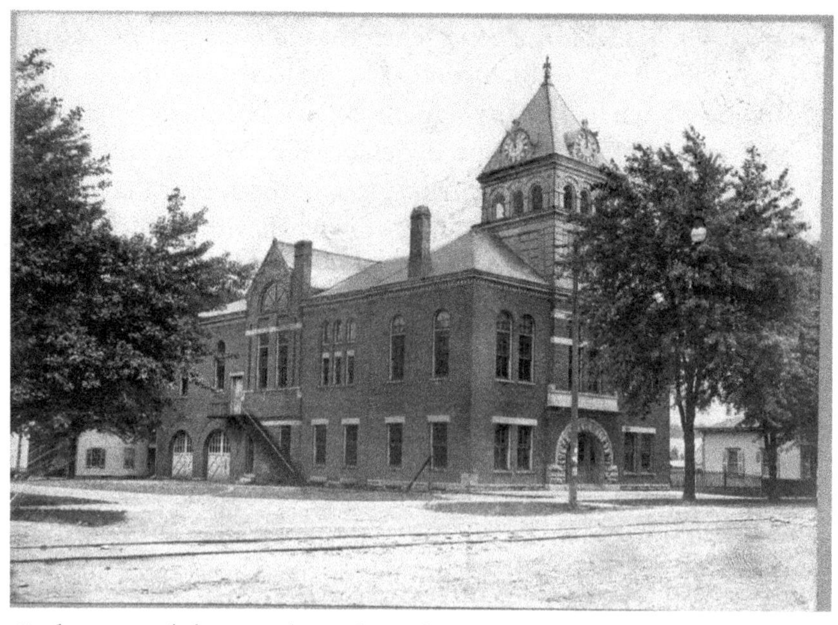

Early postcard showing the Richwood Opera House circa 1912 (colorized).

The bids for the Town Hall contract were approved by the Village Council on April 17, 1890. The total cost amounted to $8,441. The bids for the Town Hall bonds opened on May 31, 1890. The Bank of Richwood offered to pay $10,306. The purchasers of the bonds, however, went to Spitzer & Company Bankers based out of Toledo, Ohio. They offered par value and a premium of $427 with interest at 6%. The lot on which the Town Hall now stands was originally purchased by the Richwood First Church of Christ in 1880. They wished to build a larger church, but the plans were abandoned, and the lot was then sold to the Village upon which the town hall now stands.

The foundation work on the building was completed on June 19, 1890 and the festivities on July 4th included laying the corner stone of the town hall led by the Masonic Order. The Grand Master Leander Burdick gave various speeches of interest before properly adjusting and laying the corner stone. Afterwards, a grand firework show was given from the grandstand. The construction of the Town Hall was completed sometime in the fall of 1890. The Town Hall later became known as the Opera House and held many different plays, picture shows and other events for the town of Richwood. In

July 1903, it was reported in the Richwood Gazette that the town clock in the Opera House had been presented to the village by Dr. James Cutler, former president of the Bank of Richwood. The clock had been installed by Joseph Embry, a local jeweler. Mayor Hill graciously accepted the gift for the village.

Work on remodeling the Opera House started in December of 1933. Concrete was poured on the second floor of the building to create a gymnasium. The mayor's office and jail were present on the first floor of the building. At the rear of the opera house, a one-story brick building was built to house the fire department. The remodeling was paid for by the State Department and was a part of the Civil Works Administration (CWA) project during the Great Depression. The Opera House opened back up in March of 1935.

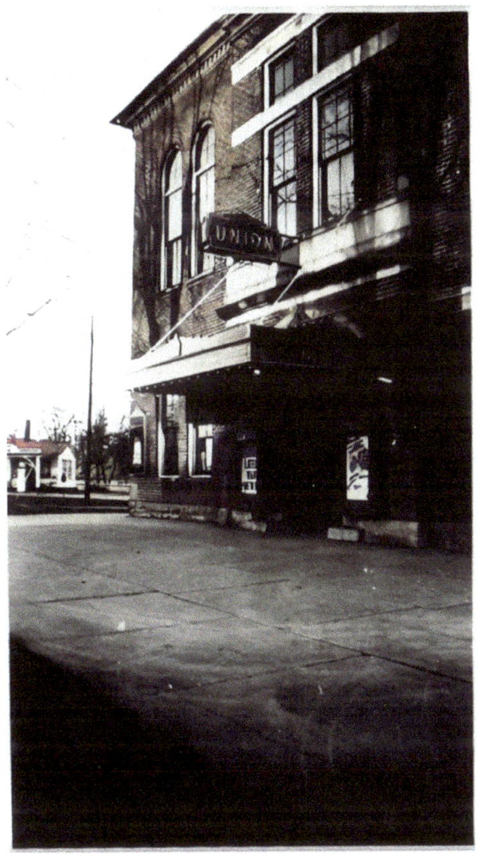

The front of the Opera House during its time as the Union Theater. Photo taken circa 1940 (colorized).

The Opera House became the Union Theater for a time around 1935 and continued to show plays and movies on the second floor to the residents of Richwood. The theater launched a drive in 1942 to sell U.S. War Savings Stamps and Bonds to moviegoers. These war bonds were essentially a loan used by the government to help fund World War 2. The theater officially closed in 1961 and its equipment, chairs and other assets were sold off. The building continued to serve as a town hall until the early 2000s when the village government moved to a house-turned-office on South Franklin Street. The fire department became a joint fire/EMS district and moved to their new facility which was built around 2001 on North Franklin Street across from the North Union High School.

The village council later purchased and relocated the town hall and police station to the old Mills Chevrolet building on the corner of North Franklin Street and Oak Street in 2009. The Opera House has remained empty and dilapidated since then. A historical marker was unveiled in 2004 to honor the history of the building. The building was designated by Preservation Ohio as one of Ohio's most endangered historic sites of 2020. Efforts are currently being led by Reddy Brown, village councilman, to repair the building and move the village government back to the former Opera House. As of 2021, plans are being made for the building to hold both the town hall and police station once more. There are also plans to establish a history museum on the first floor and a venue/community hall area on the second floor.

Chapter 10

NORTH UNION SCHOOL DISTRICT

Public education was the cause of a few people, a handful of well-connected middle and upper-class reformers, who shared one criticism of Ohio: there were too many people from too many different places but too few common values. They lobbied the legislature to create a public school system that could socialize children. Their parents may all speak different languages, and they may all have different religions but through school they thought they could create a common value system in the children. In 1821, the General Assembly permitted local districts to raise taxes for the maintenance of schools. In 1825, the legislature required people to pay property taxes to support those local schools. The legislature passed the Akron school law in 1847 which established one district for Akron with a grade system, grade levels, and one central high school and elected school board and property taxes to pay for it all. Then in 1849, the legislature extended that Akron school law to the rest of the state. Let's be clear about the underlying motive for establishing public schools: to mitigate the influence of immigrants by changing their children.

What were these values that the Reformers wanted to instill? A quick look at William Holmes McGuffey helps us figure that out. McGuffey was born in western Pennsylvania, but his family moved to the Youngstown area when McGuffey was still very young. As an adult, McGuffey served a variety of universities in Ohio including Miami University as a professor and Ohio University as its president. He is most famous for publishing the McGuffey Reader, first issued in 1836 and then revised several times after that. By the mid-1800s, the McGuffey Reader was a standard textbook across the nation and by 1890, it had sold more than 100 million copies.

The book taught both reading skills and values. For example, life was a serious business. He praised perseverance and hard work and criticized laziness, gambling and purposelessness. Character was of the utmost importance and character was exactly what your grandmother said it was. It's what you do when people aren't looking. Economic success to McGuffey was evidence of a person's good character. Most Ohioans believe that certain people were incapable of learning those lessons, so it was illegal for blacks to attend public schools in Ohio until the 1840s. It was then, in 1848, that the General Assembly finally created separate black schools paid for by the taxes of black parents. Cleveland then abolished those separate schools in the 1850s, integrating the system as did several other school districts in northern Ohio. In Cincinnati, however, the separate schools persisted. By 1860, only 38 percent of all black children attended school compared to 72 percent of white children.

Immigrant parents understood that public schools were conceived, built, and controlled by native-born white Protestants and reformists believed that civic identity as an Ohioan and as an American was far more important than any identification with religion or ethnic nationality. Because of this, immigrant parents often withdrew their children from public schools and created their own school system. A system that was usually attached to a Catholic school to teach the values that they believed in and in a language that they spoke. For example, just south of downtown Columbus is German village. On Third Street you can find the St. Mary Church built by German immigrants and a school, St. Mary School, next door to the church. Immigrant parents asked why they should give up their traditional ways.

So, there were limits to public education. It could not change everyone if only because some people weren't allowed to participate, and others chose not to participate. My point is about the construction of the public school system and the design of its curriculum. These things demonstrate for us what a growing number of Ohioans wanted to think about themselves. The school system and its curriculum represented the aspirations of Ohioans. When they compared themselves to others, especially other Westerners, Ohioans increasingly saw themselves as different.

The first school in the area was located east of Claibourne Cemetery. Around 1830, Mr. Lamphere taught children in a log cabin. Mrs. Eleazor Rose was another early teacher who lived in a two-room cabin and held classes in one of the rooms. The cabins had dirt floors, windows without glass and a fireplace made of mud and sticks. The teacher usually had no desk except for a place to store books and supplies. Seats for the students were made from split logs and made smooth by axes (although they were far from smooth—splinters aplenty).

Chores involved carrying drinking water from a creek or well and wood for the fireplace during the winter months. Books consisted of what was on hand which included almanacs, Bibles and newspapers. Teachers usually had a few readers to help out until literacy improved as time passed. Slates were used to write as well as wooden boards and charcoal markers. These early cabin schools were conducted on a subscription plan and those who couldn't afford the tax were deprived of an education.

The first school in Richwood was established in 1834, two years after the founding of the village. William Phillips taught in a cabin where the Opera House now stands. In 1835, a new log school was built on East Blagrove Street which was used until 1840. After the building became dilapidated, school was held in various churches in the area. Throughout the years, schools were built and abandoned on Fulton Street and again on South Franklin. Until 1867, the schools of Richwood constituted a township school district but in May of that year, Richwood instead became an independent school district under the law of February 29, 1849.

In 1875, a brick building was built on the site of the former junior high school located on East Ottawa and Norris Street. On January 6, 1875, a resolution was passed to ask the voters of the district the question of allowing a new building to be built. It was voted on in February and the building was erected. It was a large brick building containing eight departments. The first term began in the fall of 1876. The building was extensively renovated on in August of 1914. A new furnace and better ventilation were put in and the classrooms were updated and redecorated. Enrollment increased shortly thereafter, and faculty had trouble finding room for all the students. 125 high school students were enrolled at the time with room for only 80. The junior class went in the mornings while the high school class had classes in the afternoons. The total enrollment for the school was 410 students. The building was replaced before the second World War.

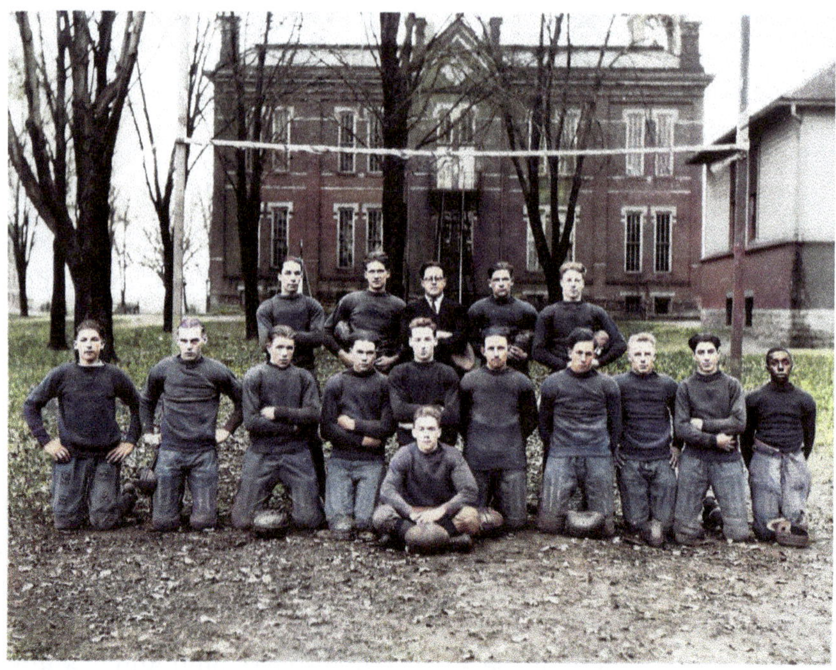

The brick school building, pictured behind this football team, was used from 1876 to 1938. It was later replaced with the junior high school building. Photo taken circa 1910 (colorized).

In 1914, various new buildings were built in the following school districts: Darby, Dover, Liberty, Leesburg, Magnetic Springs, York, Washington, and Jackson. The aggregate cost of these buildings was approximately $130,000. A bond was passed in 1915 to the amount of $39,000. The older buildings around the area were also updated and expanded upon. Uniformity of textbooks was also a matter of importance. In June of 1914, local school board members felt that they needed to slowly integrate books from a recommended list. Music in schools also made progress with a music program adopted in Richwood in 1914. Leesburg later added a program of their own the following year.

The Richwood Gazette highlighted an article in November of 1914 concerning what was known as a normal school. These institutions were created to train high school graduates to be teachers by educating them in the norms of curriculum and pedagogy. Richwood made an application to the state supervisor of normal schools to establish one in the village. The state would furnish $1000 for the normal school with the local board to furnish a place and equipment. The Union County Normal School was established in Richwood in 1915 at the same time that the public schools opened. The normal school was held in the council chamber of the Opera House until the new school building was built a year later.

The first commencement of the normal school was held on June 9, 1916. Over 200 women graduated from the school since its inception until 1926 when it closed down due to it being labeled non-essential to the school system of Ohio. The reason given for the closing of most normal schools in Ohio was that there was an oversupply of teachers. The yearly attendance at the local normal school ranged from twenty-five to thirty-five students. The normal schools that survived into the 21st century became colleges. Ohio Northern University, located in Ada, Ohio, is one such nearby college that started as a normal school.

A new high school building was erected in 1916 and contained updated plumping, heating system, and electric lighting. All rooms were finished in oak and the floors were made of maple. The bottom floor contained an auditorium which had a seating capacity of 250 along with three recitation rooms. The second floor contained a library with 125 desks and three recitation rooms. The dedication of the new building was held on February of 1917. The 1875 building was used as an elementary school which was across the street from the 1916 high school on Ottawa Street.

High school enrollment numbers expanded from previous years. In 1914, there were 453 high school students and 501 in 1915. Two new high schools were established in York Center and Jackson. The former school had 42 enrolled and the latter had 21. The past few years marked a need for schools to have libraries. The schools mostly used the State Traveling Library as well as local libraries. Outdoor play was directed by the teacher, but no organized recess was established yet.

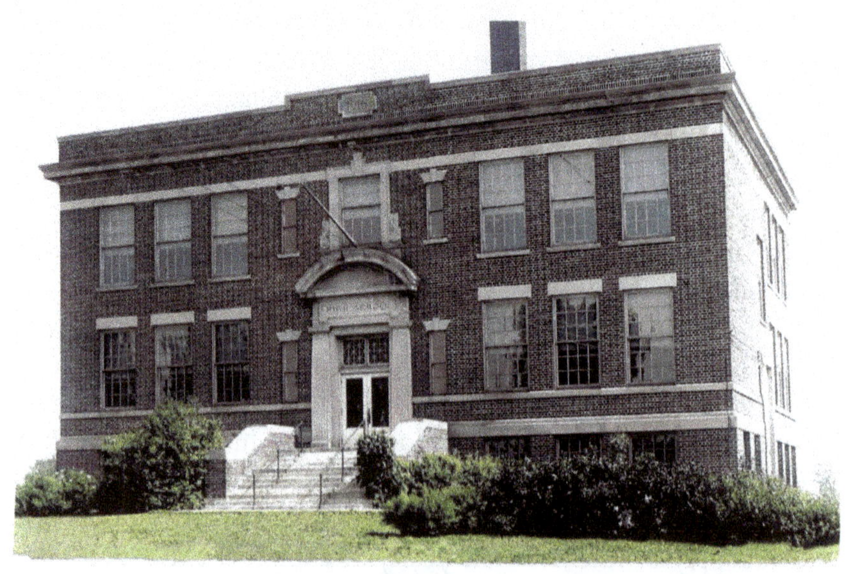

The Richwood High School building that was built in 1916 on Ottawa Street. It later served as the Claibourne Elementary school until it was torn down in 2004 (colorized).

Schools and their funding were changing by this time as well. Starting in 1914 onward, each family paid for their child to be educated. The public as well as the state would assume some of the cost. Government funding also became available around this time for early brick buildings for elementary and secondary schools. The Union County Board of Education was organized in 1914 as well. D.H. Sellers served as the first Superintendent until 1921. From 1932 to 1972, the number of high schools in Union County decreased from 15 to just 2. Consolidation of the school districts meant the schools operated 12 grades starting in 1936 and no high school should be established without an enrollment of at least 240 students. In the late 1930s, after dealing with the Great Depression, public works projects saw improvements and building projects in some township school districts. The construction of a new high school was built in Richwood with the old building being used as an elementary school. The Claibourne-Richwood School District, as it was called at the time, took advantage of the government's offer of assistance with the Public Works Administration in 1936. They wanted to build a new high school on the site occupied by the elementary school (1875 building). They commenced construction on October 15, 1938. Upon completion of the new building, the elementary moved into the 1916 building after numerous repairs. The new building housed both junior and high school students and accommodated around 520 students.

During World War II, teachers were in short supply. Among the many changes that were implemented as a result of the war, married women were finally allowed to teach. In most school districts, once a woman got married she was no longer allowed to teach. The war time period opened the door for these women to return to teaching. After the war ended, some normalcy returned.

As advances progressed in science, technology, business and industry, so too did the importance of the public school system. State planners and funders decided that larger consolidated schools could better meet the needs of students while also being cheaper. Thus, the North Union Local School District was born on December 9, 1963. The consolidated high school and junior high would be located in Richwood while the elementary schools would be: Claibourne Elementary, Jackson Elementary, and Leesburg-Magnetic Elementary. The Union County Board of Education, which began in 1914, ended on June 11, 1992 with a resolution to combine the Union County School District with the Delaware County School District. The board supported the resolution, and it was effective on January 1, 1993.

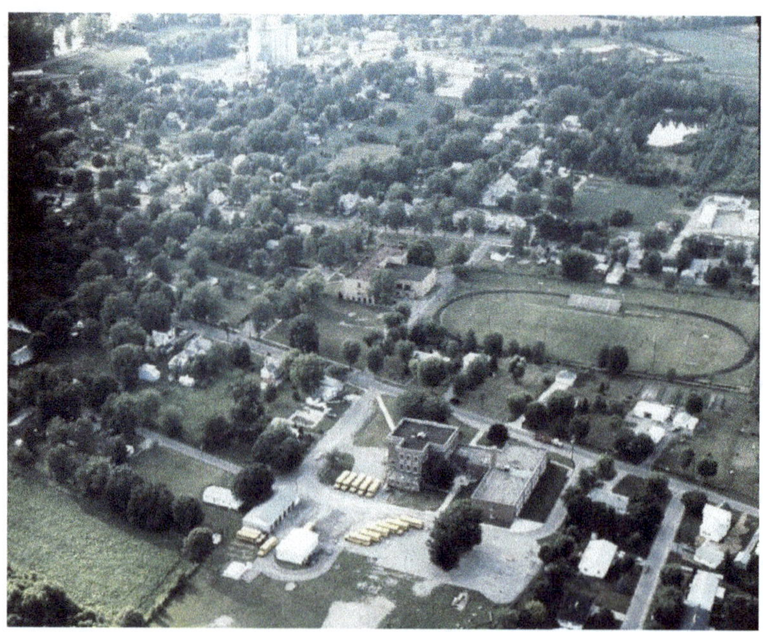

Aerial view of the 1916 building that later served as the Claibourne Elementary School (bottom right) and the 1938 building that served as the middle school (left of school track). Both buildings are now demolished. Photo taken in July of 1982.

In 1965, the Richwood and Byhalia high schools merged into one school before the school year. The freshman class had to meet in the Byhalia building until a new high school was erected. The elementary schools were also starting to become overcrowded with the 7th and 8th grade classes. The old high school (1938 building) was renovated to serve as a junior high to accommodate these classes. The North Union High School, located on North Franklin Street, was dedicated on April 11, 1969 at a cost of about $1,382,000.

By this time, all high school students were located in this new building and the Byhalia school district was closed. Three elementary schools remained: Claibourne Elementary, Leesburg-Magnetic Elementary and Jackson Elementary. Representatives from the various townships consolidated the three remaining elementary schools into one central building. The North Union Elementary School was built in time for the 2004 school year right across the field from the new high school on Grove Street. The old elementary building located on Ottawa Street was demolished. The

North Union Middle School was still operating out of the 1938 building until a new building was built right beside the new elementary on the corner of Grove and Mulvane Streets in 2008 with the old building being demolished in the process. The middle school building was paid for by the State of Ohio at about $22 million.

Chapter 11

RICHWOOD PUBLIC LIBRARY

Like so many things that meet the needs of a small community, the public library of Richwood traces its roots to a group of ladies called the Carpe Diem Club. But the idea of a library was sought after even before the club came into existence. Philip Plummer, who purchased the acreage and surveyed the land which became known as Richwood in 1832, designated a parcel of land, lot 44, as the site of a future library. The lot stood adjacent to the First National Bank on Franklin Street which, coincidentally, soon housed the Richwood Public Library in 1936. There are no records indicating the establishment of a library at that time—and it would be fifty years before one came into being—but it is interesting to note that, at a time when survival in the wilderness was paramount, the idea of a library was considered important to the future of the frontier settlement.

The present-day Carpe Diem Club was founded in 1893 after some neighbors, namely Mrs. King, Mrs. Lyons and Mrs. Tallman, would meet to read and study English literature. They found it so interesting and entertaining that they wished their friends could enjoy the same and thus the idea of a Literacy Club was conceived. This vision grew until they took action and attempted to create this club. Of course, many questions arose as to its organization such as:

How many members? Where would the meetings be held? How often would they meet?, ect.

In casting about for a meeting place, they found that a suitable room was not available, so it was decided to meet in their various homes instead. This necessitated limited membership to thirty since the homes weren't large enough to accommodate more than that number comfortably at a meeting. The meetings were held on Thursday of each week with three banquets a year. One at the opening of the Club year, one during the holiday season, and one near the close. They were held in the evenings while they entertained their husbands.

The program committee, which consisted of the organizers, made out the program for the entire year, then passing it along, when each member copied her own program. The first printed programs were called, "The Ladies Literary Club." However, some of the members wanted a better name and several were submitted to the committee. The name "Carpe Diem" was selected. Mrs. King gave that name as it was once used by the club to which she belonged in Dayton, Ohio. It literally means "Seize the Day" in Latin. The club interpreted it as "Improve the Day or Time," as the object of the Club was to broaden and enrich the social and intellectual life of women, to keep them in touch with the present, to help them clean from the past and garner for the future. Miss Corna Comer—Sister of Mrs. King—was the first president of the Club. She held the office for three years.

As the Carpe Diem Club grew, so did the need for its members to lead discussions and programs on challenging topics. Members were assigned a topic to research and present to the group; afterwards each presenter would lead a discussion. A sample from meeting minutes in the 1890s included: English literature such as Sir Walter Scott, Robert Browning and John Milton, as well as histories of England and France, the study of mythology, American history from 1850 to 1895, the rise and growth of Mormonism, and a comparative study of Parliament and Congress.

The resources for carrying out the research necessary for these topics were few to nonexistent. Challenges in the physical environment were present as well since most homes were lit by coal-oil lamps. Because of this, it was an effort to read and study for lengthy periods. The streets were also unpaved at this time which made moving around difficult. There were no automobiles yet and horse and buggy were the main modes of transportation. Despite these challenges, the women of the Club were determined to overcome these deterrents to their studies and find a way to supplement their reading material—they saw a need for a public library. There were periods when the club's efforts were fruitful, and times when its members diverged from their goals. But the story of their success is one of commitment and perseverance.

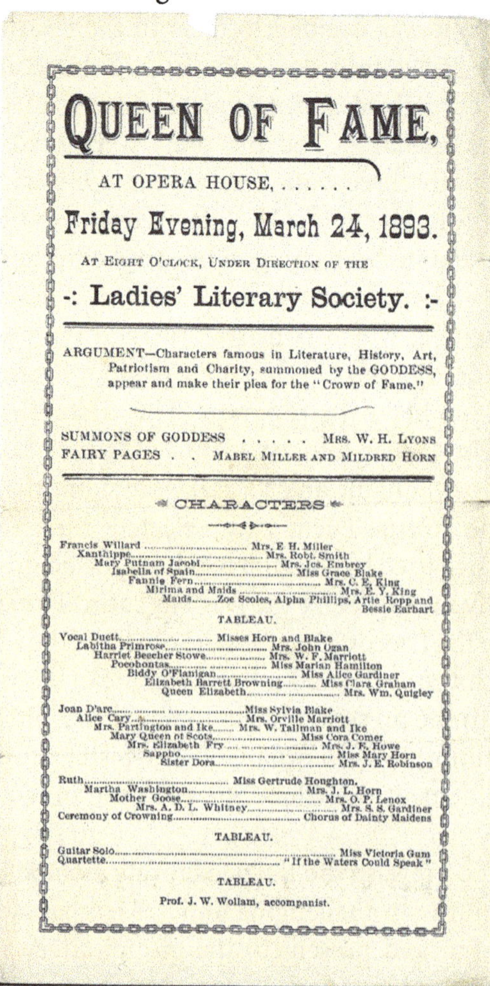

QUEEN OF FAME,

AT OPERA HOUSE, ...

Friday Evening, March 24, 1893.

AT EIGHT O'CLOCK, UNDER DIRECTION OF THE

-: Ladies' Literary Society. :-

ARGUMENT—Characters famous in Literature, History, Art, Patriotism and Charity, summoned by the GODDESS, appear and make their plea for the "Crown of Fame."

SUMMONS OF GODDESS . . . . . MRS. W. H. LYONS
FAIRY PAGES . . MABEL MILLER AND MILDRED HORN

CHARACTERS

Francis Willard .... Mrs. E H. Miller
Xanthippe .... Mrs. Robt. Smith
Mary Putnam Jacobi .... Mrs. Jos. Embrey
Isabella of Spain .... Miss Grace Blake
Fannie Fern .... Mrs. C. E. King
Mirima and Maids .... Mrs. E. Y. King
Maids .... Zoe Scoles, Alpha Phillips, Artie Ropp and Bessie Earhart

TABLEAU.

Vocal Duett .... Misses Horn and Blake
Labitha Primrose .... Mrs. John Ogan
Harriet Beecher Stowe .... Mrs. W. F. Marriott
Pocohontas .... Miss Marian Hamilton
Biddy O'Flanigan .... Miss Alice Gardiner
Elizabeth Barrett Browning .... Miss Clara Graham
Queen Elizabeth .... Mrs. Wm. Quigley

Joan D'arc .... Miss Sylvia Blake
Alice Cary .... Mrs. Orville Marriott
Mrs. Partington and Ike .... Mrs. W. Tallman and Ike
Mary Queen of Scots .... Miss Cora Comer
Mrs. Elizabeth Fry .... Mrs. J. E. Howe
Sappho .... Miss Mary Horn
Sister Dora .... Mrs. J. E. Robinson

Ruth .... Miss Gertrude Houghton.
Martha Washington .... Mrs. J. L. Horn
Mother Goose .... Mrs. O. P. Lenox
Mrs. A. D. L. Whitney .... Mrs. S. S. Gardiner
Ceremony of Crowning .... Chorus of Dainty Maidens

TABLEAU.

Guitar Solo .... Miss Victoria Gum
Quartette .... "If the Waters Could Speak"

TABLEAU.

Prof. J. W. Wollam, accompanist.

Advertisement for the "Queen of Fame" presented at the Opera House on March 24, 1893 by the early Carpe Diem Club.

Their first step was to launch a fundraising campaign by staging entertainment at the Richwood Opera House. One Friday evening on March 24, 1893, they presented the "Queen of Fame," during which each Club member portrayed a noted person such as Martha Washington, or Harriet Beecher Stowe. Funds from the entertainment helped support a "reading room" where books could be housed, and tables and chairs were available for reading and writing. The Club's meeting minutes help us locate several sites in Richwood which were used as "reading rooms."

The first site, selected in 1895, was a small building on the land in which the present extension of the current library building now stands. The Claude Swartz Ford Dealership, and later, the Bill Ford Dealership occupied those lots for many years. In 1896, the Carpe Diem Club lobbied the Village Council to provide them with a space in the City Building, free of charge. The request, however, was denied. In April of 1897, a group referred to as the U.M. Club would allow two of their rooms to be used for a reading room as long as the Club paid half the rent of $3 a month. The Club agreed on this arrangement.

It wasn't until 1910 that the idea of a public library resurfaced. The Carpe Diem Club appointed member Mrs. James Cushman as Club librarian. In that same year, the Club's Civic Committee gave a report evidently supporting the establishment of a library. The Club voted to approve the report and to pursue a public library project. Significant steps were taken in March of 1911 to advance the library project. The Carpe Diem Club secured a room from the City Building, located on West Ottawa Street, to be shared with the youth of the Young Men's Christian Association. Miss Mae Harriman, who succeeded Mrs. Cushman as the Club librarian, was to be in charge of activities of the room. Under her management, the fledgling library blossomed. The husbands of the Carpe Diem Club members began to be involved—their ability to generate broad support provided much-needed momentum and financial support for the library.

The first library board was formed and organized on January 26, 1915. The officers were: Rev. J.R. Lloyd, President; A.R. Klipstine, Vice-President; Mrs. C.E. King, Secretary; and Mrs. Charles Snowden, Treasurer. Other members included: Dr. Herman C. Duke, L.J. McCoy, and retired school superintendent, A. Oliver. Faced with the need to expand, the new board found that the only rooms available were on the second floor of the Hastings Building on Franklin Street. The building was a three-story structure located beside the Richwood Banking Company. The Franz Millinery Shop occupied the first floor. The rent was set at $6 per month. Following discussion, the rooms were rented for 13 months at $75, and the board agreed to cut an opening for double doors and to paper the rooms. Mae Harriman was hired as the first official librarian of the Richwood Public Library.

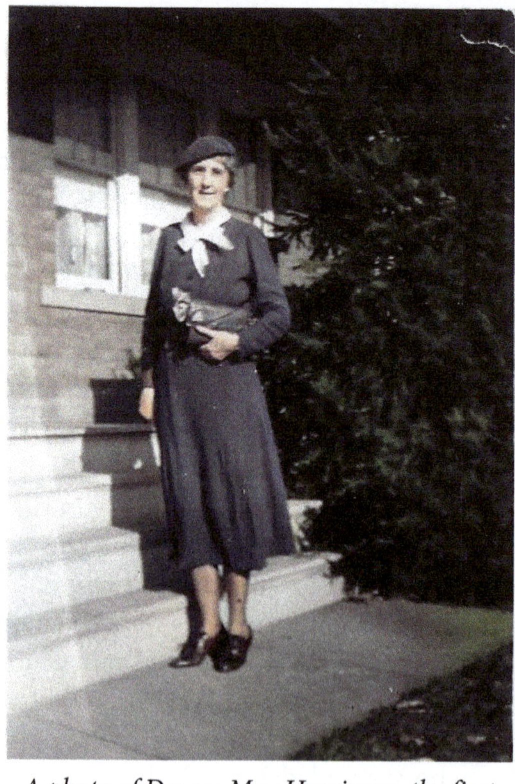

A photo of Donna Mae Harriman, the first librarian of Richwood circa 1920 (colorized).

On the afternoon of April 3, 1915, a Book Reception was held in the new library rooms. Rugs, a stove, a table, 150 books and $12 in cash were donated. According to an article in the Richwood Gazette, it was reported that this first public library had 635 books with 150 loaned from the State Library of Ohio at its formal opening on April 15, 1915. It also held subscriptions to popular periodicals and a large collection of old magazines.

Legal documents verified the transfer and the sale of the Vaughn Building to the library in 1917. It appears that the library moved to this building which was located on East Blagrove Street behind the Richwood Banking Company. A Mrs. Copp purchased the building for $859, with the stipulation that the library be housed on the first floor, and a museum on the second floor. As far as we are aware, the museum was never established. The library board voted to purchase the property for $1,080.

By 1921, the library was flourishing. Miss Nora Lake was the librarian and earned a salary of $18 per month. The library board and its officers remained the same. A significant change occurred, however, in 1925. The Ohio State Legislature placed libraries under the Department of Education. The Richwood Public Library became a "school district library." Geographically, the borders of the school district also determined the service area of the library. From 1925 on, the local Board of Education assumed responsibility for appointing the Library Board members. Permission to go on the ballot to raise money for the building also had to be approved by the Board of Education. From this day to the present, the school and library have worked together to provide resources for students and teachers.

Everything was moving along great until the Great Depression hit in 1930. The community rallied to give support. The Carpe Diem Club, although no longer involved directly with the library, took an active role in helping to maintain the institution which has become important to the village. In March 1932, each member donated 25 cents to the library. With thirty members, this meant that they contributed a total of $8.25 which was one-half of Miss Lake's monthly salary. By October 1933, the library's affairs had become troubled. The Club canvassed the town, asking for donations of books for the library. They were also advised that Miss Lake was behind many months of her salary. The Library Committee of the Carpe Diem Club would work with the library trustees to correct the situation. In December, they voted to send a letter to every resident in Richwood requesting donations of money or books. The letters were hand delivered by boys from the elementary school.

The Depression, for all its hardships, offered opportunities for the library. By 1935, the effect of the Depression had closed the First National Bank, which was located on the east side of Franklin Street. Mr. L.J. McCoy, who had been in close contact with the bank, was also on the library board. He helped facilitate the opening of negotiations to buy. The library board offered the bank $2,000 but the bank rejected that offer. The board raised the amount to $2,500 and on March 24, 1936 the sum was accepted. Payment was made by $1,000 in cash and the procurement of a loan of $1,500 from the Richwood Banking Company. The records show that by May 6, 1936 the plans to remodel the small but imposing pillared bank and equip it to house a library were well underway.

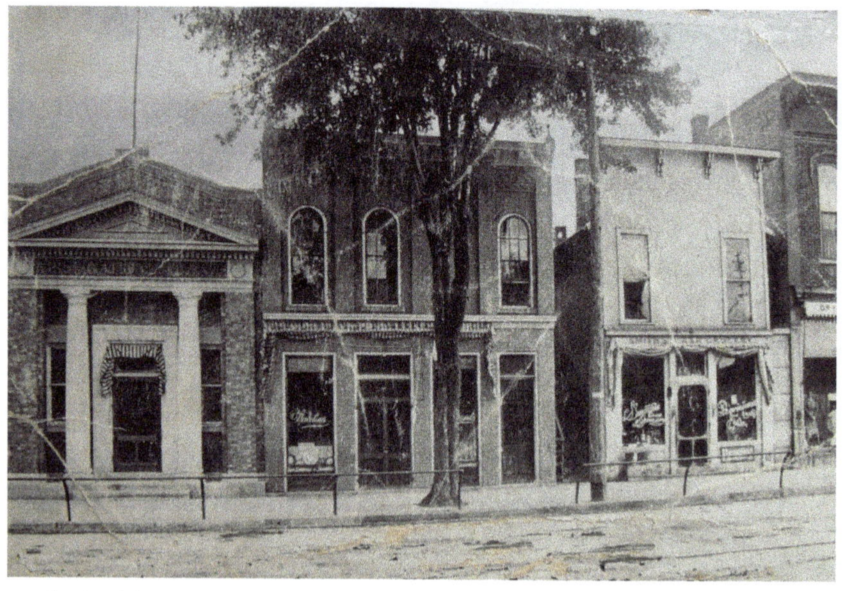

The building on the left served as the Richwood Public Library after the First National Bank closed down during the Great Depression.

This location served the community well for many years. After Miss Lake retired, Mrs. Louise Peet became the librarian. Mrs. Mabel Vandergriff was the next librarian, and she was assisted by Mrs. Cuma McDaniel. After Mrs. Vandergriff's retirement, Mrs. McDaniel became the librarian. Her dedication to the library inspired it's growth to the point where a new location was necessary. The library board established a fund to construct a new building. By this time, the funding of the library was provided by the intangible tax collected at the county level, some of which could be set aside for building purposes. A gift of residential property on East Blagrove was sold, and that money was added to the fund.

Finding a suitable site for the new library posed a challenge. The only available site was a property on North Franklin Street that was formerly Benton's Garage. It was purchased by the board who discovered at a later date that it was unsuitable for a number of reasons. Fortunately, the board was able to sell the property, and, when the East Ottawa location became available (after an oil company decided not to purchase it for a filling station), it was unanimously agreed to be the best possible location.

The library board hired the architectural firm of Edwards, Burris, Lockwood of Marion to design the new building. James Hafer, a librarian from Newark, was hired to work with Mrs. McDaniel in the selection of library equipment and furnishings as well as to assist with the general layout. The location was purchased in July 1971 for $15,000. The bond levy, which came up for vote in the North Union School District, passed easily. The final cost of the building was $165,735. Furnishings costed around $22,326. The library was dedicated on September 22, 1974. The board members gave great consideration to the naming of the new building. Since the school district's boundaries were expanding, the library was serving a larger community. The board members, therefore, approved the new name: The Richwood-North Union Public Library.

Mrs. Judith A. Lawler was hired in 1981 to succeed Mrs. McDaniel as librarian. There were five other members on the paid staff. Students and other community members volunteered their time and services. Members of the library board at this time were: Frankie Stults, President; Mary Kerns Howard, Vice President; Jean Wedding, Secretary; Dr. Steve Hockett; and James A. Blue. Ruth Robinson was the Clerk of the Board.

The new library grew and expanded as they continued to meet the needs of the community. The Web Plastic building and lot on East Ottawa Street was purchased and used for community meetings and extra parking for the library. Under Mrs. Lawler's stewardship, the old card catalogue became automated, and the first computers were installed. An Open House was held at Christmas and Santa was there to meet and greet those who attended. The Art Club of the local North Union High School also displayed their work at the library during Springenfest. Both of these traditions continue to this day. The library expanded onto the current building in 2004. The expansion included a kid's room, magazine room, video room and the extensively used community meeting room.

Mrs. Lawler retired in 2010 after 29 years of service. Sarah Moore was hired by the library board following Mrs. Lawler's retirement. Sarah received a Bachelor of Arts in Psychology from the Ohio State University in 2005 and a Master of Library Science degree from Indiana University in 2007. She and her staff continued to increase participation in the facilities and in the programs offered by the library: a local history and genealogy room, programs and events for children, teens and adults, public computers and Wi-Fi access.

In 2012, the library joined the Serving Every Ohioan consortium. SEO provided the library with extensive access to over 8 million items by linking around 100 library systems for resource sharing across the state of Ohio. In 2008, the library had been coping with a 28% cut from the State's Public Library Fund. The library reduced its staff and hours of operation by 27% and severely cut the operating budget. The board decided they should ask the community to support a levy on the November 2013 ballot. The resolution was approved by 69% of the voters in the district. The library was able to restore their hours after it passed.

2015 saw the beginnings of a new volunteer organization called The Friends of the Library. The organization intended to nurture and support the work of the library moving forward. Such support harkens back to the early days of the library when a group of friends sought to foster intellectual stimulation and social gatherings in the village. Sarah Moore resigned as Director on February 14, 2018 with Audrey Deel taking up the role in March of 2018. The library currently employs a staff of around seven people who have continually improved the building and its services. It continues to be largely used by the local community and remains a valuable resource for the village.

Chapter 12

LAKE BACCARAT

The Richwood Lake is a beautiful addition to the village and greatly improves the surrounding area. The lake was previously known as Lake Baccarat and was originally a gravel pit owned by various companies throughout the years. The area of Richwood is known for containing much gravel which was widely sought after in the construction of railroads, roads and other projects. During the Civil War, ballast was dug from this gravel pit originally owned by Susan Swartz and was located north of Graham Lane. This street, at the time, crossed Lynn Street and ended on Franklin Street. Gravel was taken in small quantities until after World War I when large lots were dug up. After the war ended, many roads were starting to be built to accommodate the automobile boom. Gravel started to become a prized commodity.

There was a small crusher at the site of the pit at one point until the owner went broke. The local kids would swim there until it started being used as a dump. A large pond was formed that became known as Barnes Pond. About 1900, Mr. Sieg leased this land from the railroad to get gravel from the local roads. This operation quit about 1910 until the year 1919 when Jesse Kagey & Co. bought the Swartz pit and the land to the south which is now a part of the park. They started to dig on the south and east sides of the lake. A Mr.

Krouse was hired by Mr. Kagey to build a dredge boat from the local lumber. A large crusher was also built. The dredge was powered by a steam engine and had a scoop arm that was 14 feet long. It would push against the bottom of the pit with a scoop and was held in place by two large spuds that pressed against the bottom.

A small railroad track was built with cars pulled by a farm tractor. The digging was located along the east side of the lake with the dredge digging its own path as it moved north. Gravel was hauled along the tracks to the crusher where large iron rolls crushed the coarse gravel into road gravel and sand. The sand was carried to the front of the lot near the road by a large bucket which moved on a high cable. The bucket was pulled by cable by a donkey engine at the crusher.

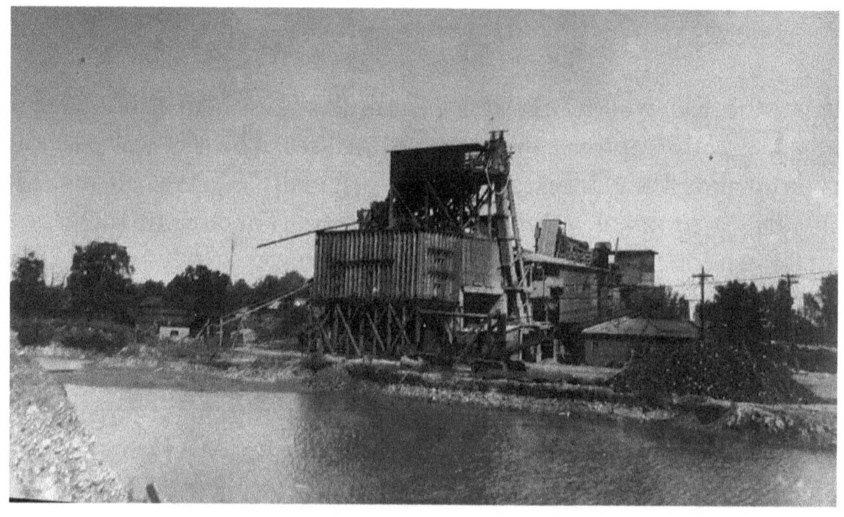

The large crusher at the Richwood gravel pit circa 1920 (colorized).

The dredge continued to dig west as it dumped the overburden back into the lake behind it. Gravel from the pit was used to build many local roads and continues to serve as the foundation for our modern roads. Trucks loaded the gravel from bins at the crusher and the sand from huge piles at the front of the lot. The lake originally extended south to Grove Street until the central part was filled in by drainage from the crusher and became a swamp. This left the large lake and the little lake which was later filled to make the current baseball diamond.

The last order for gravel was used in the foundation of State Route 31 that connects Kenton and Marysville. The order was completed in 1934 and all work at the pit ceased in 1937. The company fell on hard times due to the depression and the appearance of quicksand on the east side of the lake. The land was later sold to the National Lime & Stone Co. until the business folded in 1937 and everything was torn down.

Lake Baccarat opened as a place of recreation in the summer of 1924. The community shared the site with the gravel pit. Those who swam in the lake managed to stay clear of the dredge and the movement of gravel from the pit to the crusher. Lake Baccarat was the name chosen when it officially became a lake. The lake was named after our local American Legion Post Baccarat, Post #40, which was organized in 1919. They took over what was left of the coasting hill and made room for a bath house and swimming hole. At the grand opening of the lake, they had swimming races and a high diver which stood 30 feet above the lake.

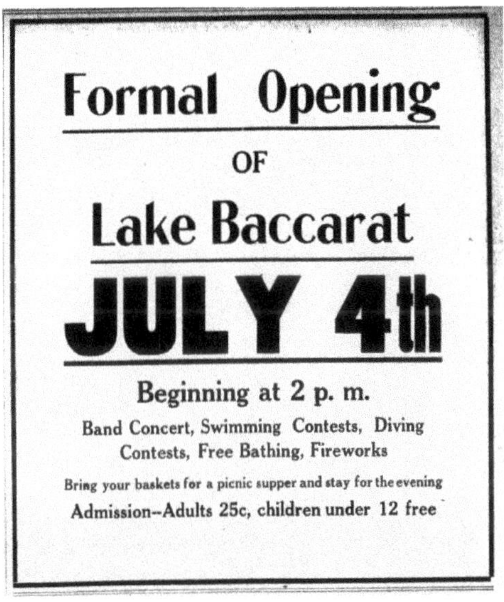

Advertisement in the Richwood Gazette featuring the opening of Lake Baccarat in 1924.

The land was later deeded to the state in 1942 and became a state park. The name was changed to the Richwood Lake and a shelter house, toilet facilities and recreation area was built. In 1951, local citizens led by Charles Brobeck developed a beach and swimming area using donated funds. The Richwood Village Council took over the lake and appointed a Park Board who governed the operation of the lake. The board was in charge of hiring lifeguards and general maintenance of the area. The ball diamond was built by the Richwood Lions Club in 1956 at the cost of about $2500. They also provided Park Day dinners until their disbandment in 1994. A shelter house building was built in 1961 at about the same price as the ball diamond. In the 1950s to the 1960s, swimming lessons were given at the beach and were sponsored by the American Red Cross of Marion. One of the swimming instructors was Mary Ellen Withrow, who later became treasurer of the United States under President Bill Clinton.

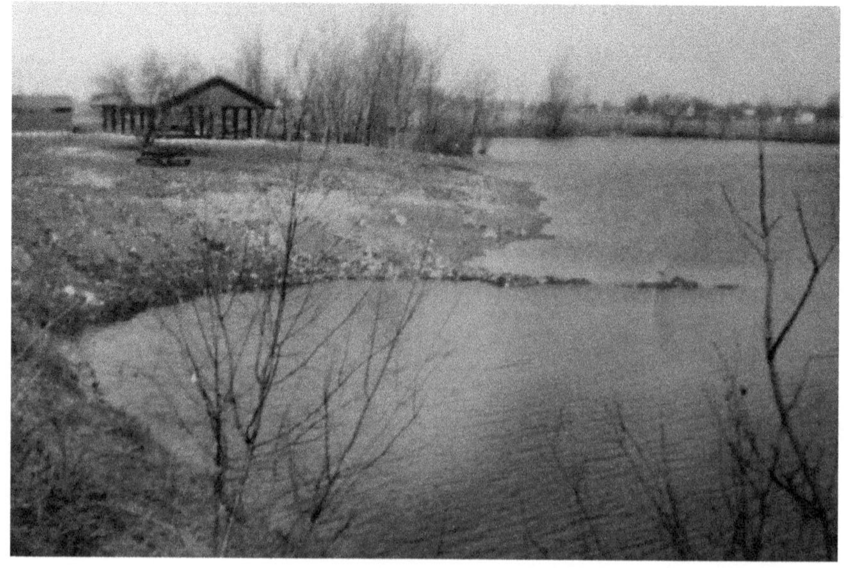

The beach at the Richwood Lake was developed in 1951-1952. Photo taken circa 1952 (colorized).

1961 also saw the construction of a kiddie pool which is currently no longer there. The Kings, Daughters & Sons and the Essex K. of P. Lodge were responsible for picnic tables. The Jackson and Claibourne schools filled the mosquito swamp and turned it into the current ball field. The park was leased from the state until 1982 when the state gave the land back to the village. At this same time, the park day program was created and included tons of fun programs including pioneer craft demonstrations of the old days. The profits of this program raised about $40,000 to be used for improvements at the park and lake.

The last park program celebrated the Ohio Bicentennial in 2003. An Amish built gazebo was built in 1997 and a North Union District

Veterans Memorial was unveiled at the Richwood Lake in 2004. After years of rain and flooding, the banks around the lake started to erode the natural trail away and exposed many of the roots of the trees that line the banks. In 2017, a group of locals called the Trail Blazers decided to do something about it. Members of this group composed mainly of the parks committee for the Village of Richwood.

Together with the village council, they applied for various grants including the Ohio Department of Natural Resources to provide financial assistance for public recreation purposes through the Recreational Trails Program. They were able to procure $1.9 million in grant money through the Ohio Department of Natural Resources Trail Funds and Ohio Capital Improve Fund along with $250,000 through capital improvement, $150,000 through Ohio Department of Natural Resources trails and the village itself which was able to use roughly $100,000. The money went toward several improvements such as rocks to line the banks to prevent further erosion, two new properties for parking lots at the softball fields, and a 10-foot-wide walking path. The project completed at the end of 2018. Further improvements were made including a newly built shelter house and improved beach.

Many drownings have unfortunately happened in the lake throughout the years. One man named John Allen drowned on August 20, 1937. John was 26 and worked as a carnival employee. He accompanied Marian Chapman to Richwood to attend a funeral of her mother. Both were employed together as members of a carnival company that played in Richwood over the Fourth of July weekend and were supposed to have been married on the day that he drowned. The young man was attempting to swim the quarter mile width of the lake with another companion, Frank Miller. Allen either became too exhausted or suffered a heart attack. Frank was unable to rescue the man and called for help. Allen was rescued from the lake by a man who was nearby. A physician was called and worked over the body for more than an hour but to no avail. Authorities failed to locate any relatives of the man and his remains were placed at the vault in Claibourne Cemetery in the hopes relatives would later be found. There is no record of his interment.

Chapter 13

TROLLEY & INTERURBAN

Richwood had its own trolley and interurban railway situated downtown from 1907 to 1918. It became big news after the word came out in 1906 that the budding village could possibly have an electric railway running through it. A company by the name of Pittsburg Co. built the railway north through Essex and LaRue to Findlay. It would then connect with a line that ran from Toledo to Fort Wayne. The plans were made to use Strang Line gasoline-electric cars. They were powered by a gasoline motor of 110 horsepower and a generator which connected the batteries and driving wheels. They required no overhead trolley and ran at a speed of 60 mph.

On April 13, 1905, President John G. Webb and General Manager George Wysal were in Marion and stated that Chief Engineer Williams of their road was looking into the feasibility of a new route to Richwood which would entirely do away with the necessity of figuring with the commissioners on the question of bridge rights. The proposed new route would branch off from their line south of Newman's bridge, crossing the river diagonally and striking the road which runs west from the river about midway between Prospect and Newman's. The plan was to run the track across the river on piles, but the greatest objection to the plan was the danger from ice gorges.

The river had a rocky bottom which would make pile driving difficult, and it would be something of a job to build it enough to be out of danger from the ice. Newman's bridge itself was another proposed danger. It was considered unsafe and, during a flood, was liable to be washed down the river.

On Aug 8, 1906, W.H. Ogan, promoter of the Lima, Kenton and Marion Traction Company, stated that their work was about to begin on the line. He urged the people of Richwood that if they wished to have the line extended to LaRue and Richwood from the Lima, Kenton and Marion Line, that $30,000 needed to be raised. He promised that if successful, the work will begin within ten days after the amount was raised. The farmers of LaRue had managed to raise $15,000 and were ready to do business with Ogan. The people of Richwood were urged that if they wished to have the interurban built to send any amount of money to B.L. Talmage at the Richwood Banking Co.

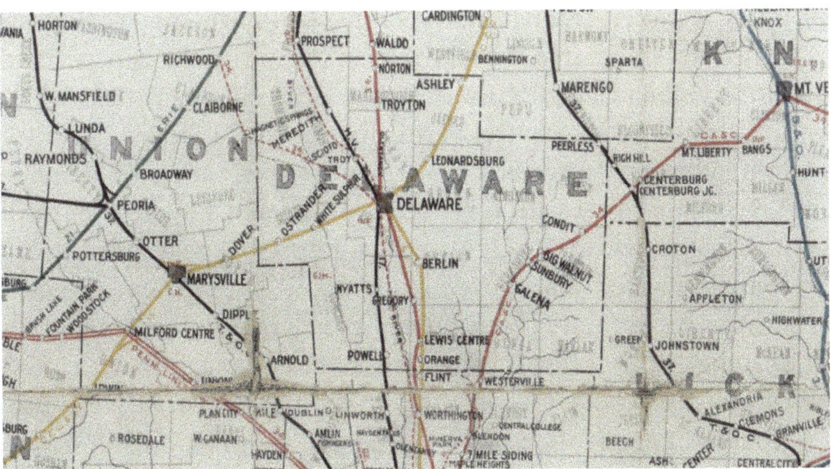

A map of the railroad systems in Ohio in 1910. The red dotted line marked with the number "34" represents the electric railway. The line extended to Richwood from Delaware. The green line represents the Erie Railroad that also passed through Richwood.

The money was successfully raised, and work was to begin on extending the line into Richwood. On January 31, 1907, Richwood residents were surprised to see an Erie freight train running south through the center of Franklin Street over the C. M. S. & N.

interurban track. The locomotive pushed several cars of the railroad south on Franklin Street to the end of the track. Agent Johnson of the Erie Railroad, several members of the construction crew for the interurban line, and many others were on the train. At every house along the line, doors and windows were open as the people of Richwood observed the amazing sight. A temporary connection between the Erie Railroad and the interurban remained for several years.

Many property owners on Franklin street along with numerous businessmen met with the Village Council on March 7, 1907, to discuss whether Franklin street should be paved with brick or macadam. It was a necessity that the street would have to be widened since there was only about five feet for vehicles to run on either side of the track. The question was whether they should invest more in paving the street with impacted stone to better enhance the beauty of the town. There were around 100 citizens at the council meeting to express their feelings on the subject of improving Franklin street which became a free-for-all debate. A majority of property owners in the residence district of the street desired a macadamized street while those in the central part from the Opera House north to the railroad wanted a paved street. Those north of the railroad preferred a macadam street with it properly graded and widened so it will be in proper shape for traffic after the interurban line was finished. The council decided that they would employ a competent engineer to furnish an estimate of the cost of paving, macadamizing, grading, curbing, ect., of Franklin street from one end to the other. The street committee would look into it providing the cost of the project wouldn't be too much.

The Village Council hired James C. Kennedy who was known to have improved many streets in Marysville to survey the street and come up with estimates. Mr. Kennedy was instructed to proceed with the work as soon as he was able. W.H. Lyons of Richwood sent a letter into the Gazette proclaiming that he is not in favor of macadamized streets. He referred to Mt. Vernon Avenue in Marion which was macadamized for three years before they tore it up and put asphalt down instead. The man explained that they couldn't stand the dust it made and replaced it. According to Kennedy's estimates, a 36-foot street with 8-inch compact gravel foundation, first-class vitrified brick with concrete filler and a 5-inch sandstone curb set and reinforced in concrete could be made for $3.05 per lineal foot on both sides of the street. To build a first-class macadam street of the same width with cement gutter, it costed $2.70 per foot on each side of the street. After months of heated debate, stubborn council members, and high bids, it was finally passed that the south of Franklin street would be paved with vitrified brick with the rest being paved with crushed stone macadam.

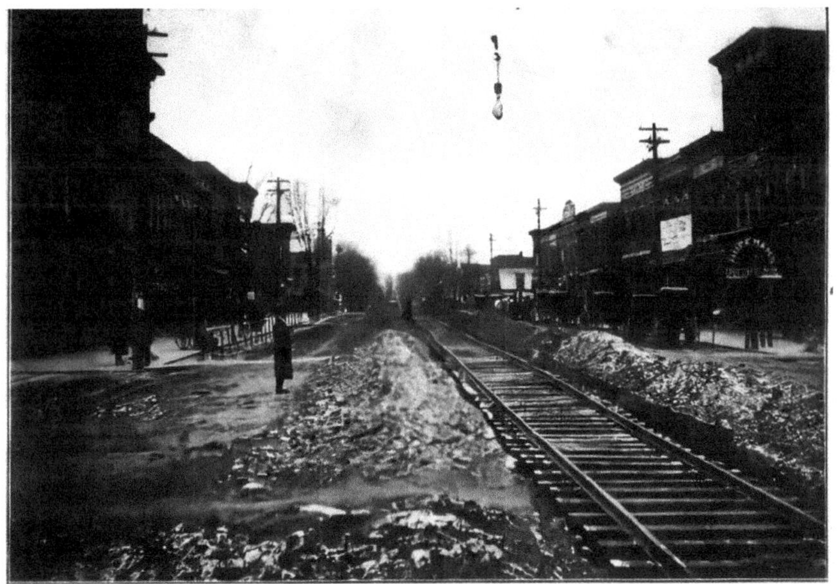

Franklin Street looking south during the construction of the Interurban circa 1906 (colorized).

The Village Council met in June to discuss the interurban railroad company and their actions. A motion was unanimously passed asking the company to fix up Franklin Street which was impassible and was completely occupied by track. The motion also stated that the line must be completed and in operation within the next ninety days or the franchise which the company owned would be declared null and void. Sometime in the summer, the Springs Construction Company, under the management of W H. Ogan of Indianapolis, went bankrupt causing investors to lose a lot of money. Mr. Ogan was compelled to give up his scheme of constructing an electric line from Columbus to Kenton via Delaware, Magnetic Springs, Richwood and LaRue. Everything remained dormant after Mr. Ogan's failure, for several months, until the Delaware and Magnetic Springs company, with H.E. Buck as manager, took up the task of completing the road to Richwood by the end of the year. The company offered 17 cents an hour, $1.75 for a ten-hour day, as they tried to finish before winter.

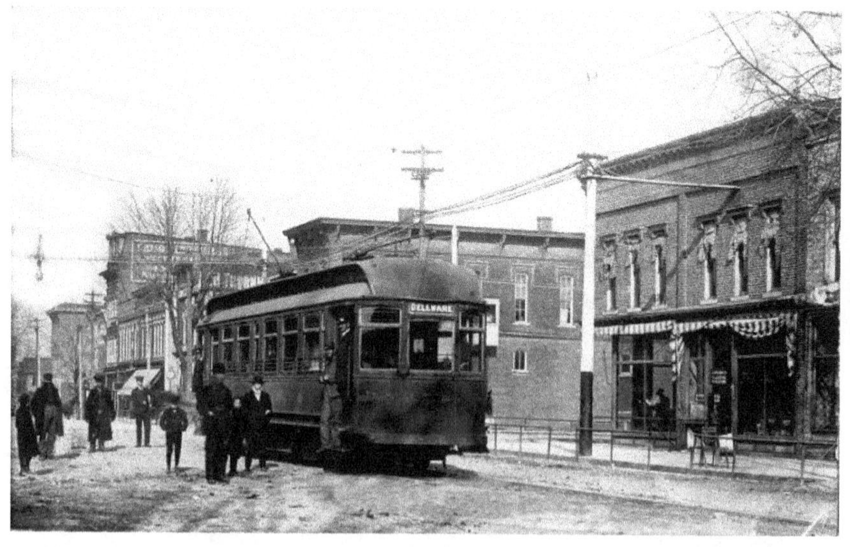

This photo was taken in front of the Clark and Gaston Store and was furnished by Charles Evans, a former employee of the interurban. It is presumed that this was taken when the line made its first run on Thanksgiving day. (Colorized)

The first car on the interurban arrived on Thanksgiving day, 1907. Mr. H.E. Buck had the honor of completing the road and running the first car over the line on Thanksgiving day, with Frank Mitchell as motorman and Bert Loveless as conductor. The car was greeted by a large crowd but could not run any farther north than the creamery on that day. It arrived at the creamery at 9:30 a. m. and was soon well loaded with people who were determined to take a ride, some going to Magnetic Springs and others to Delaware and on to Columbus via the C. D. & M. The men working on the road were kept busy every hour constructing the trolly line and Saturday at noon announced that the first car to run through the business center of the town would make its appearance at 4:30 P.M.

Franklin street from the Erie depot south was filled with people anxious to get a peek at the first car, which arrived exactly on time and had been running on the following schedule: Leaving Richwood— 6:20, 8:50 and 11:50 a.m., also 1:50, 4:20 and 6:20 p m. and on Saturday at 8:30 p.m. The conductors were Frank Mitchell and William Hanson, the motormen, Frank Mitchell and J. V. Hildreth. Mr. Loveless had been advanced to agent at Richwood. The temporary depot at Richwood was on South Franklin Street, formerly occupied by Mill's used car lot in the 1980s, where a neat and comfortable waiting room had been constructed for the patrons of the road. The fare from Richwood to Magnetic Springs was 10 cents, from Magnetic Springs to Delaware 30 cents, round trip from Richwood to Delaware 75 cents, round trip from Magnetic Springs to Delaware 55 cents, and round trip from Magnetic Springs to Richwood 20 cents.

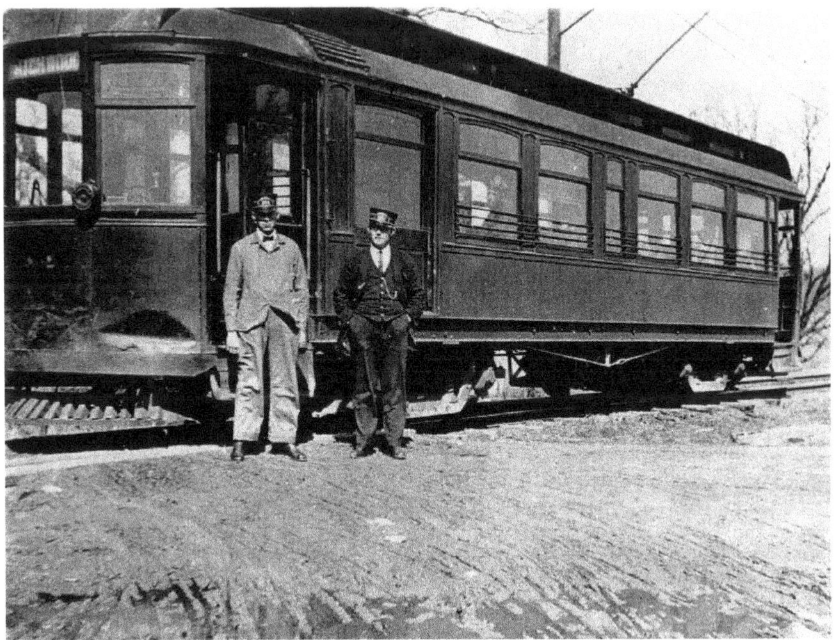

A photo of one of the trolleys from the Columbus, Magnetic Springs & Northern line. Their next stop was at Richwood as displayed by the sign in the front. Photo taken circa 1910 (colorized).

The first and only accident of the interurban led to the death of a woman by the name of Eliza Jane Love, aged 82 years old, on June 23, 1911. She had been visiting the home of friend, Mrs. Fuller, of South Fulton Street and walked to the home of Mr. and Mrs. Scott Hanawalt who lived just beyond the end of the South Franklin Street paving. She left the paved street and was walking beside the car track when George Murphy, in charge of the work car, approached from the rear. Murphy, seeing the aged woman, blew his whistle to warn her that the car was coming. Had she remained where she was, her life would've been spared. Instead, she became bewildered in seeing the car and stepped in front of it. It was sudden enough that the motorman didn't have time to stop the car.

Murphy, who was badly grieved by the affair, stopped the car and rushed to her aid. She was still breathing but had been badly injured. Going to a nearby telephone, he called Manager C. J. Fifer who rushed to the scene of the accident in his automobile. The two men lifted the unconscious woman into the car and hurried to the office of Dr. Roebuck. By the time they reached their destination, she was no longer breathing. The coroner of Union County pronounced her cause of death to be accidentally struck by the C. M. S. & N. car. Interment was made at the Claibourne Cemetery.

The Great Flood of 1913 caused incredible damage to the state including the interurban. About 93 people were killed in Columbus with hundreds more killed in Dayton. Dayton was covered in fire since the flood waters prevented firefighters from getting to the buildings. The flood wiped out many bridges across the county including the bridge at the Claibourne Cemetery and the Scioto River bridge. Money was tight enough as it was thanks to the automobile industry taking away business. The Pennsylvania investment company, that owned the electric railway, was reluctant to repair a lot of the damage. Much of the cost fell to locals to raise money for the repairs.

For a few weeks, no traffic was moved along the railway. Once the track was rebuilt and the Fulton Creek bridge was repaired, a single streetcar began to run from Richwood through Magnetic Springs to the river. The car was used as a locomotive as well to move freight cars. At the Scioto, a boat had to ferry people across the river to get on another interurban so that they could continue to Delaware. Eventually, they built a footbridge to walk across the Scioto to get to the train. The bridge over the Scioto was eventually repaired and business resumed. The company abandoned the line, and the last car ran for the last time on December 31, 1918. The tracks were later used by the Erie Railroad to help deliver coal and freight to Magnetic Springs. A further attempt was made to revive the interurban in 1919 but it did not reach fruition.

Chapter 14

RICHWOOD FAIR & EVENTS

Richwood has always had a large part when it comes to horse racing. The track located at the fairgrounds was known as one of the best in the state. Morris Hill built the track on his own land and sold it to the fair association in 1892. That same year, the first tri-county fair was held. Hill later became mayor of the village. Nate Spratt, known as being one of the oldest working blacksmiths in the area, owned a famous horse named Civilization. The stallion sired many local racers and won over $9,875 with a total of 110 races. He was buried in the infield of the racetrack, in the southeast corner of centerfield, after his death in 1906. Two other racehorses are also known to be buried there, Malcomb D., owned by the Cheney Brothers, and Exandu, owned by Harold Besst.

The fair association was formed by a group of racehorse owners who bought the racetrack from Morris Hill. Five additional acres were purchased, giving the grounds around 35 acres and access from two different roads. An agricultural exhibition was presented for the first time in October 1892, along with three days of horse racing. In one of the races, a horse named H. B. M., driven by Lou Seeseholtz, took the bit in his teeth and, in trying to regain control of the horse, Seeseholtz broke both reins. A resulting collision threw him to the track, and he fractured his ankle and bruised his body. After the collision, H. B. M. finished the race in style, taking first place. The Gazette mentioned how spectacular it was to watch the driverless horse complete the race, passing all others to take the lead. The horse, however, was disqualified from the race due to lack of a driver.

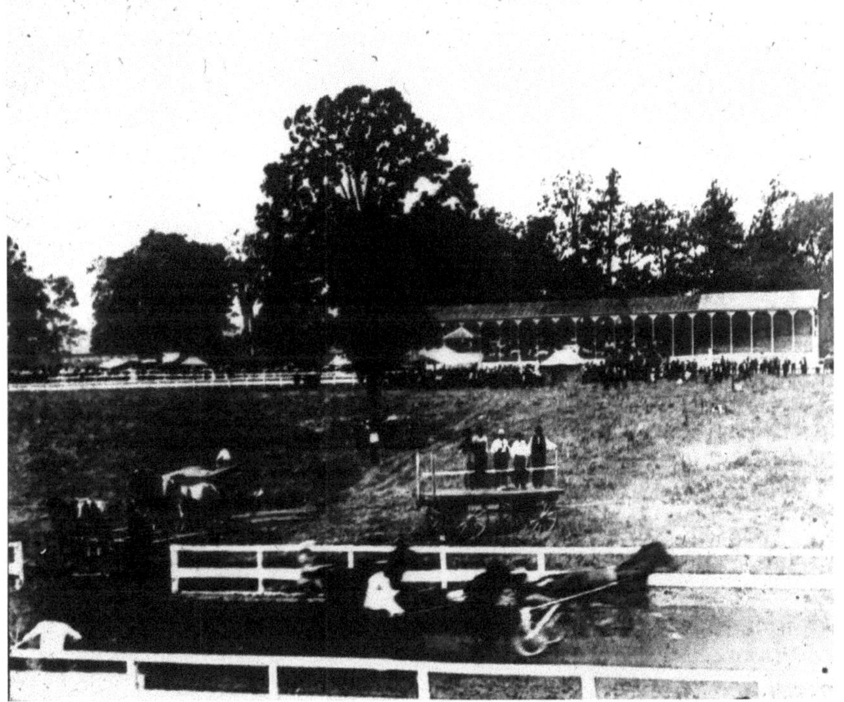

Horse racing at the Richwood Fair Grounds circa 1900.

A premium book of the Seventh Annual Fair, which was held in October of 1898, revealed many interesting business advertisements and the various animals and crops for sale. Premiums were offered for more than seventy kinds of farm fowl including forty of chickens, turkeys and ducks. Field crops included four kinds of corn and three of wheat as well as rye, barley, oats, flax, clover, peas and lima beans. A full dinner was offered for 25 cents by E. E. Moore's bakery and F. O. Penney's bowling alley and pool room, with the latter also offering a snack of beefsteak, bread, and butter with coffee for 15 cents.

The booklet reveals that an ordinance was passed that year to add stone sidewalks on the streets and electric lights would be working for fair visitors. Advertisers in the book included Webb & Hayes, who sold used schoolbooks at 110 North Main Street (Franklin Street) and The Eagle Drug Store, located at what became the Heritage Restaurant, offered buggy paint for 70 cents and stock feed for 35 cents. F. W. Simmons, a veterinary surgeon and dentist, advertised his animal hospital on North Main Street and invited fair goers to leave their horses at his stables. Two local flour manufacturers, The City Mills and Brick Flouring Mills, also advertised their flour and gave premiums at the fair for bread made from it.

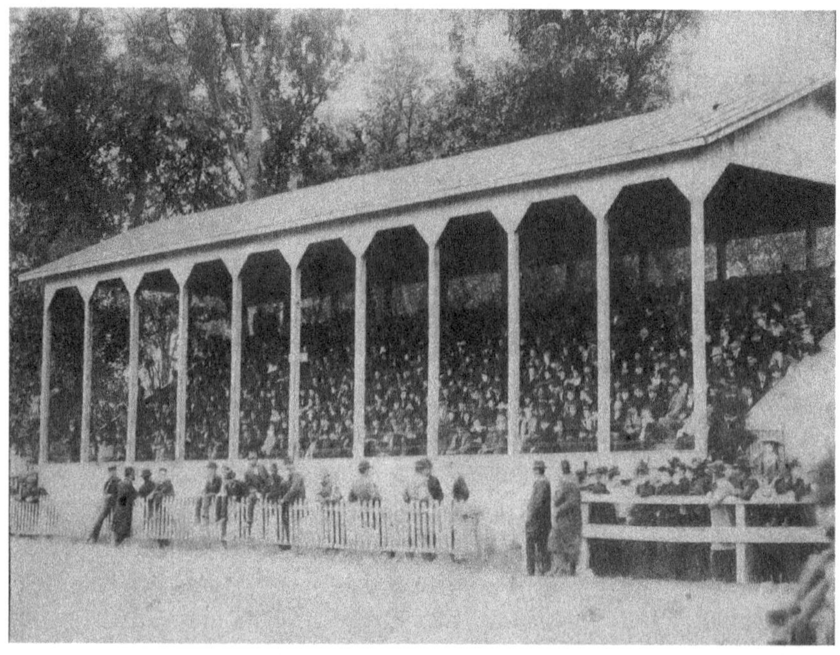

The grandstand full of people at the Richwood Tri-County Fair. Photo taken circa 1910 (colorized).

Today the Richwood Independent Fair continues its festivities over labor day weekend with horse races, games, rides, children and senior day, 4-H and F. F. A. exhibits, livestock sales, a demolition derby and concerts. It is one of only a few independent fairs still operating in Ohio. Harness racing continues to be important in Richwood. One of the largest wholesale and retail outlets for blacksmith supplies in the area is Ken Davis & Sons, Inc., located in Richwood on East Blagrove Street (Route 47). The Ohio Quarter Horse Association has established their state headquarters here in Richwood as well since 1995.

* * *

In 1965, the Civic Center hosted a large event that borrowed the best from many different acts. This event, which they called the Richwood Civic Center Equarnival, hoped to capture the thrills of a horse race, the action of a Rodeo, the atmosphere of a carnival and the enchantment of an Indian festival. The sum total of all was found in this event which was held at the Richwood Fairground on June 18 and 19. Championship cattle cutting approved by the National and Ohio Cutting Horse Associations was one of the main attractions for Friday and Saturday evenings. Timed horse contests and a rodeo was also held that Friday night.

Saturday's entertainment was filled with exotic Indian dances and Princess Beverlee, a 15-year-old television and musical show performer, who presented various Indian Dances. Princess Little Pigeon with her four young warrior sons performed the war dance and Chief Little Fox gave demonstrations in fire eating. White Cloud performed feats with his dart gun when he is not playing the drums. Princess Beverlee (of Apache heritage) was the youngest dancer to be named to the Indian Hall of Fame. Many Indian Hobby and Novelty stands featuring Indian craft and wares decorated the midway. The carnival atmosphere was created by the presence of the Steinmetz Amusement rides and games and Harold Baker Pony Rides. A Quarter Horse show featuring halter and performance classes was also held.

The Equarnival was sponsored by the Civic Center to further its local civic works. The show committee consisted of Calvin Wells, Lester Krebehenne, Fred Inskeep, Stan and Lee Sobas, Jim Smith, Carroll and Jerry Fogle, Lee and Ann McCaferty, Lowell Parker, Charles Shearer and W. P. Drake. The refreshment stand was under the direction of Marie Hamilton and Rev. John Wagner. Rev. Carroll Bickley was in charge of gate admissions while Mrs. Gladys Cheney was in charge of registrations. Sportscaster Jimmy Crum was on hand, acting as Master of Ceremonies as well as announcer. Dr. W.

P. Drake put hour upon hour as well as his own money to plan for the Equarnival. The total income from the event was close to $3,700 dollars, out of which all bills were paid, and 20 percent of all profit went to the Fair Board for use of the grounds. The Civic Center netted approximately $1,000 for its use at the Center.

* * *

The United States Bicentennial Celebration in Richwood took place from Friday, June 11 to Sunday, June 20, 1976. Local businesses held a sidewalk sale on the first day to kick off the celebration. That evening, a street dance was held in the downtown business area. The dance was sponsored by the American Legion Auxiliary with Helen Collier serving as chairwoman for the dance. The "Stringalings" of Marysville provided the music. The local 4-H clubs combined to sponsor an old-fashioned ice cream social during the dance. The next day festivities included the bicentennial parade, sponsored by the American Legion Post 40. The parade included floats, antique cars, bicycles, the North Union Band, an old-fashioned circus calliope, Marion Cadets, Marion Jets, a Frontier Militia from Mansfield, the Douce Dancers and many others. Also, that day was an art exhibit and sale and a craft show at the Richwood Middle School.

The next day, on June 13, a chicken barbecue was held at the Richwood Lake, sponsored by the Richwood Lions Club. The club also hosted a day of fun which included games and contests. For people of all ages as well as a concert by the Civic Center Kitchen Band. Flippo the Clown also made an appearance at the barbecue dinner. The highlight of the day, however, was a tug-of-war across the Richwood Lake between the Lions Club and American Legion Post 40. The celebration also included fireworks, a free outdoor movie, a demolition derby contest, harness racing, and a bicentennial parade.

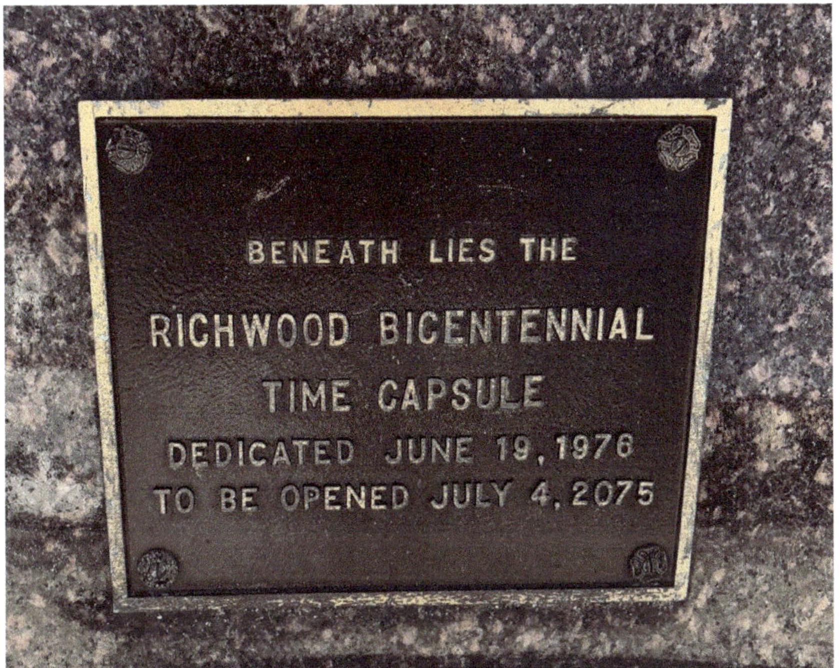

The plaque located in front of the Richwood-North Union Public Library. The date is mistakenly displayed as 2075 instead of 2076, the actual date of the Tricentennial.

Perhaps the biggest event that still remains today, was the burial of the Richwood Time Capsule. The capsule was buried on June 19 at 2 p.m. in the courtyard of the Richwood Public Library. A fee of five dollars was charged for each item placed in the capsule the size of a shoe box with all proceeds earmarked for a civic project. The capsule itself was properly sealed and placed through the efforts of Ed Stofcheck and the Alexander Wilbert Vault Co. of Mansfield. The time capsule is scheduled to be opened on July 4, 2076 in celebration of the nation's Tricentennial. Once opened, plans were made to auction off the items with 20% of the proceeds to go to the Richwood Public Library. The capsule was sponsored by P.A.R.T. (People Active in Richwood Today).

* * *

Street fairs were a common occurrence in Richwood since its inception. The Richwood Springenfest was a local street festival that began in the 1980s as a way to raise money for the North Union

Athletic Committee. When it first started, Franklin Street was closed off for people to walk around, listen to music, and eat at various food stands. Games and other entertainment were also present. The festival was held each year sometime in June. Over the years, the festival became less of a street fair and more of a fundraiser as attendance dwindled. It became harder to find volunteers and gain as much revenue as they did in the past. After more than 30 years and over $400,000 raised, it had run its course in its original state. Eventually, after a brief stint at the fairgrounds, the Springenfest was rebranded. In 2018, the NUAC held a Springenfest Sun Run 5K/2M Fun Walk utilizing the newly built Richwood Lake trail. In 2019, the Richwood Sports Festival made its debut which became one of two other races in Richwood; the other being the Ruth Woods 5k Run/Walk sponsored by the Richwood Civic Center. Attempts have been made to establish a street festival again but so far they have not succeeded.

* * *

In 1982, Richwood celebrated its Sesquicentennial from July 29 to August 1. The celebration included programs on Richwood's history, a large 3-hour parade, street dance, and "A Day at the Park." Displays were set up around the village that year pertaining to the history of Richwood in one way or another. A letter from Governor James Rhodes was also published on July 13, 1982 congratulating the village. Various souvenirs were sold including plates, key chains, T-shirts and belt buckles. Charles Barry and Freda Kyle served as Sesquicentennial Co-Chairmen.

A narration review of slides and music, headed by Richard Cline, was held at the Junior High School (the 1938 building) on July 29 and July 30 that looked back at the history of Richwood. Local residents took part in pioneer costume wearing for the occasion. A tour of the old homes in Richwood was also given with the present owners serving as hosts. That afternoon, a large parade passed through Franklin Street. Floats that depicted Richwood history, antique cars, and bands strolled down the street to the many residents and visitors.

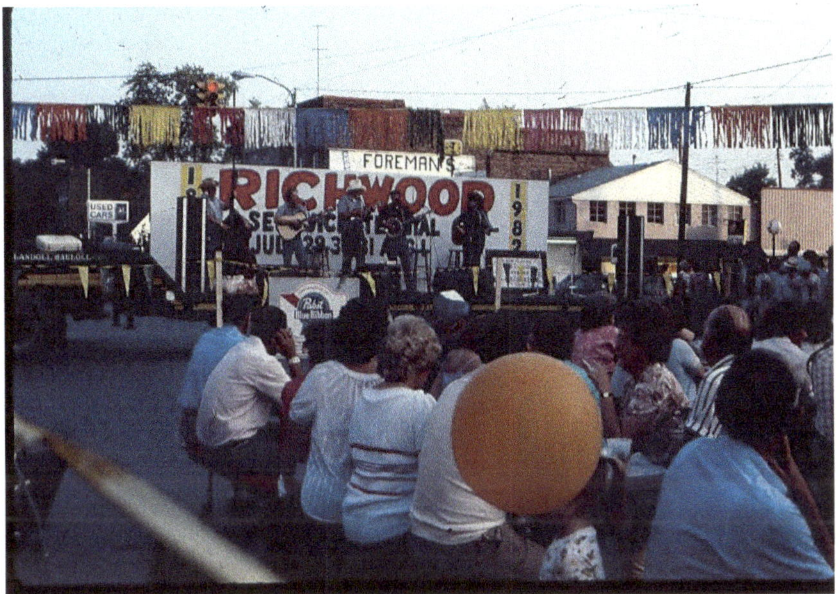

The Bokescreek Blue Grass Band playing on Franklin Street during the Richwood Sesquicentennial. Photo taken July 31, 1982.

The Bokescreek Blue Grass band played in the evening for a street dance of old-fashioned square dancing. On the final day, Ruth Cowgill coordinated stage entertainment and pioneer demonstrations at the Richwood Park. Dubbed "A Day at the Park," a festive scene ensued with various people dressed in pioneer clothing of the 1800s. The place resembled an authentic look at what it was like during the era of Richwood's founding. Among the demonstrations were butter making, basket weaving, quilt makers, blacksmiths, and candle making. Musical entertainment included the Civic Center Kitchen Band, Marionairs Barbershop Chorus, Clowns, and Cord Razors Quartet.

Chapter 15

ADDITIONAL PICTURES

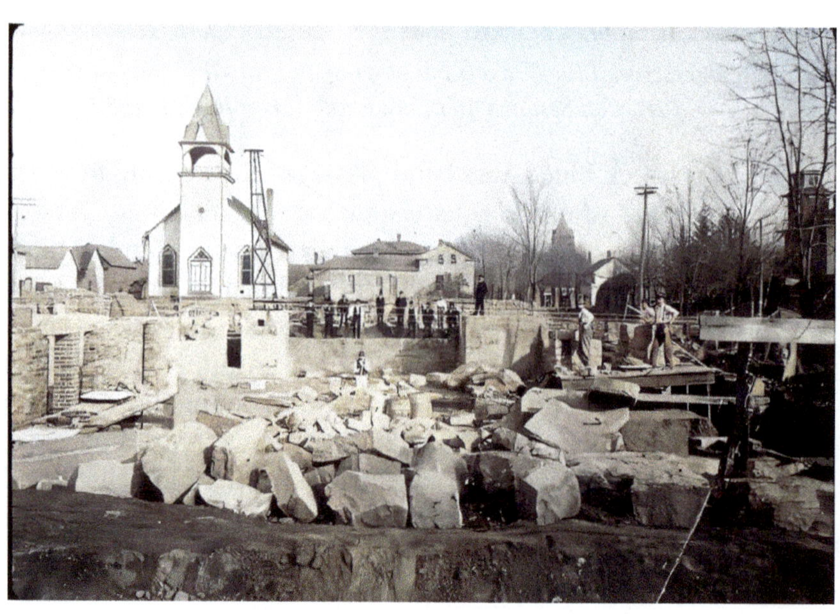

Construction of the Methodist Church on Fulton Street, in the same spot where the old M.E. Church was located, which was completed in 1902 (colorized).

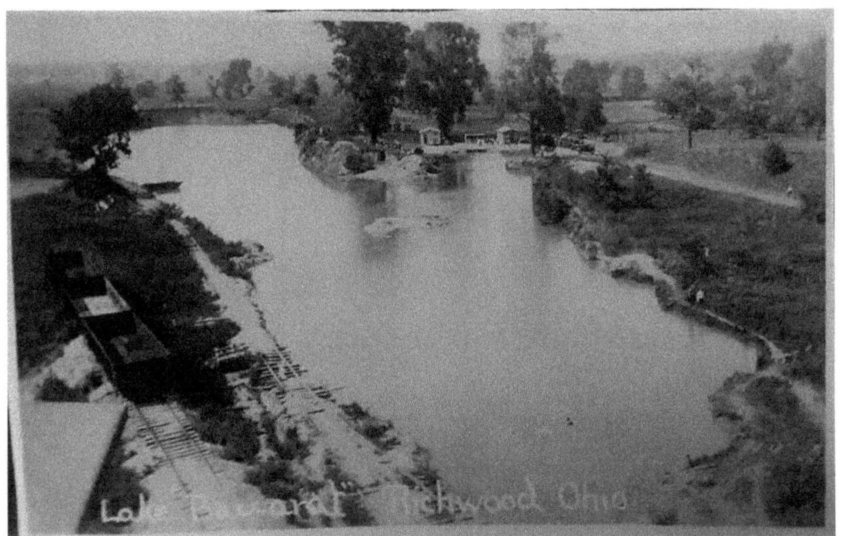

Aerial view of the gravel pit in Richwood circa 1920.

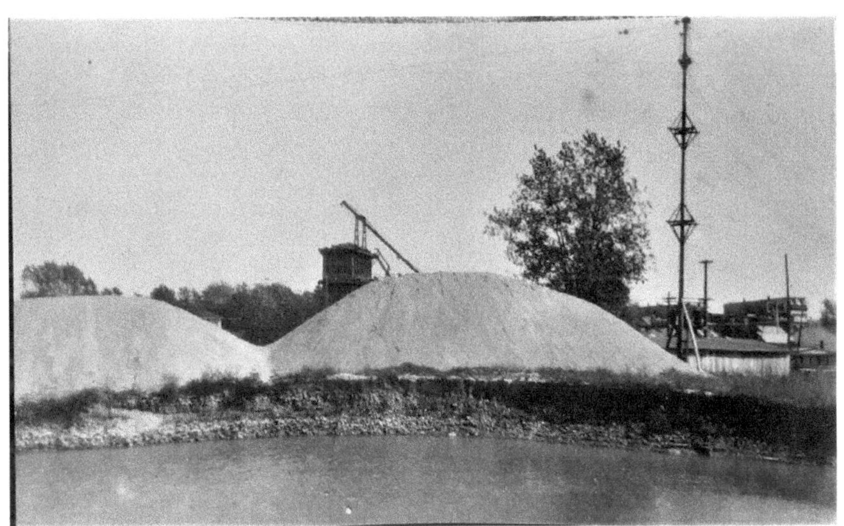

Another view of the gravel pit circa 1920. The mounds of sand can be seen piled in front of the crusher (colorized).

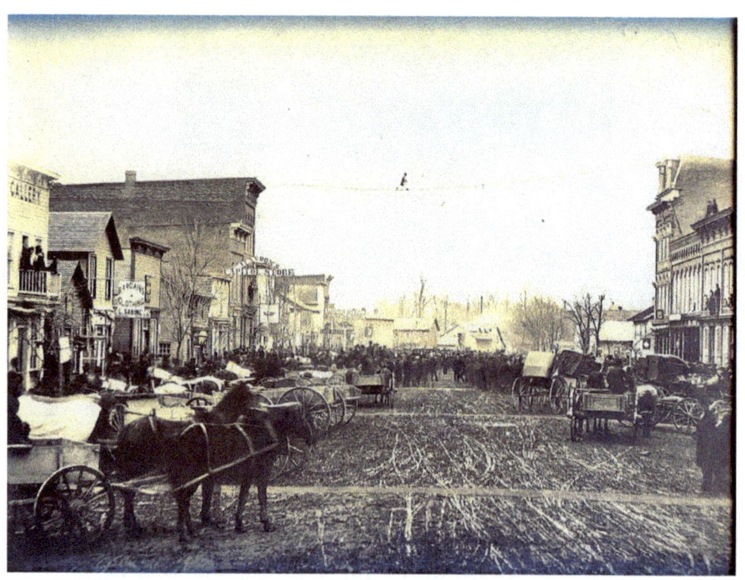

Photo of the Fourth of July celebration in Richwood in 1876. Notice the man walking along a tightrope above Franklin Street.

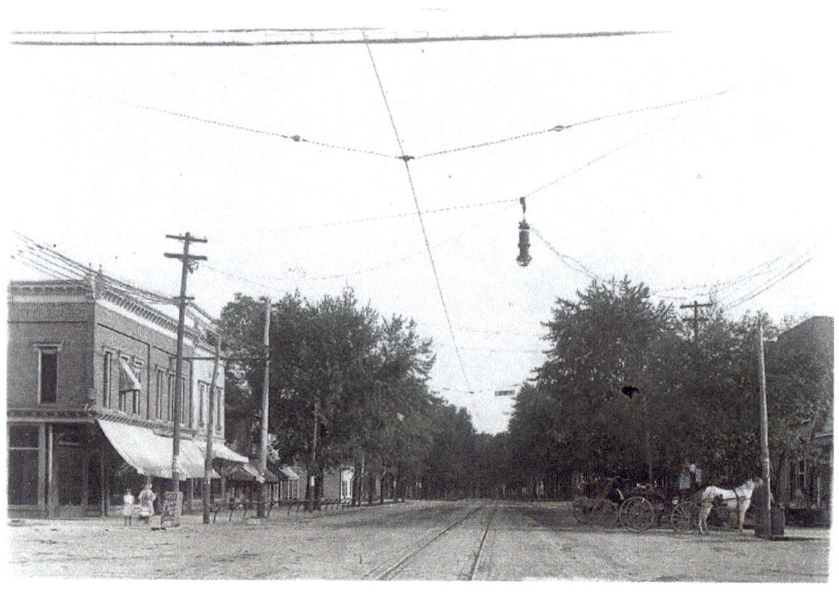

Intersection of Ottawa and Franklin Streets looking south. Photo taken circa 1912 (colorized).

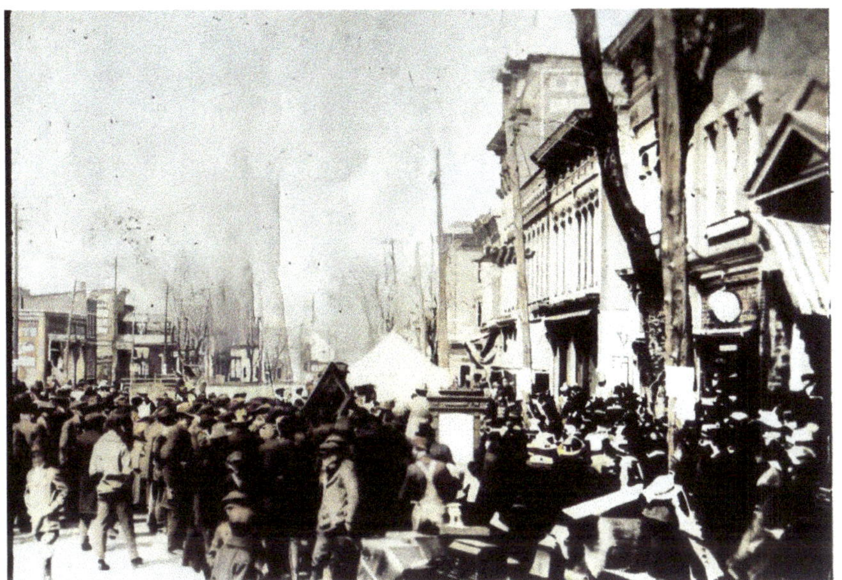

Auction taking place on Franklin Street during World War I to help raise money for the war effort. Photo taken circa 1917 (colorized).

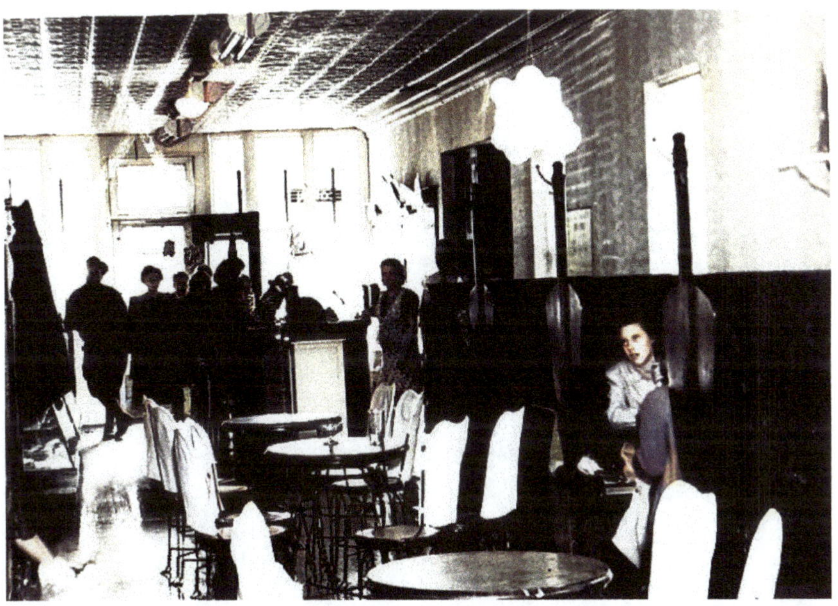

Inside the Chiesa Bros. Ice Cream Parlor located on Franklin Street. Photo taken circa 1930 (colorized).

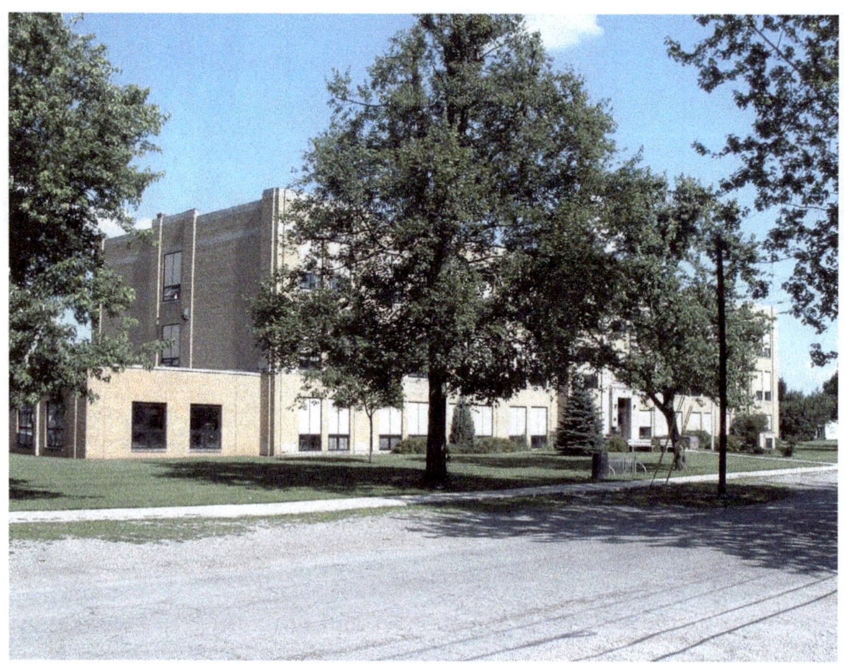

The 1938 building located on Ottawa and Norris Streets. It was later demolished in 2008 after serving as the junior high for numerous years.

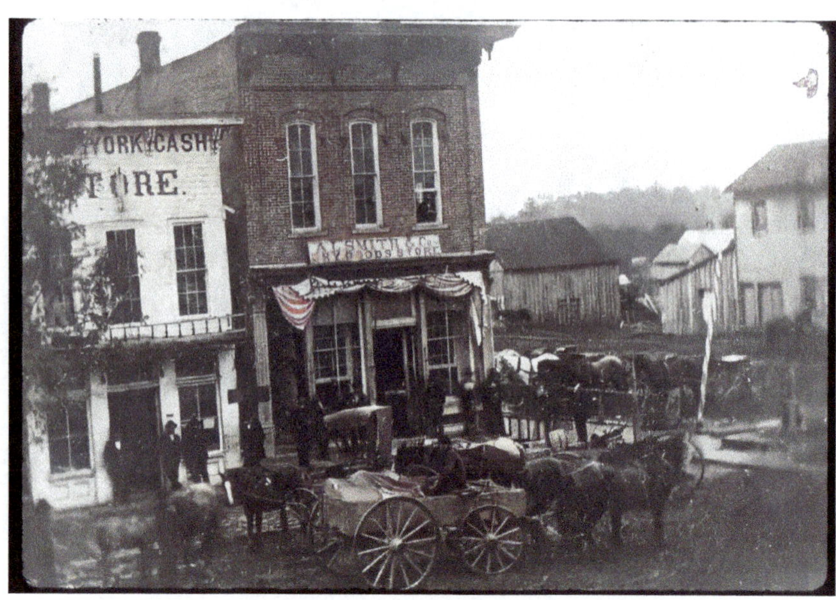

Corner of Franklin and Ottawa Streets looking east. Photo taken circa 1870 (colorized).

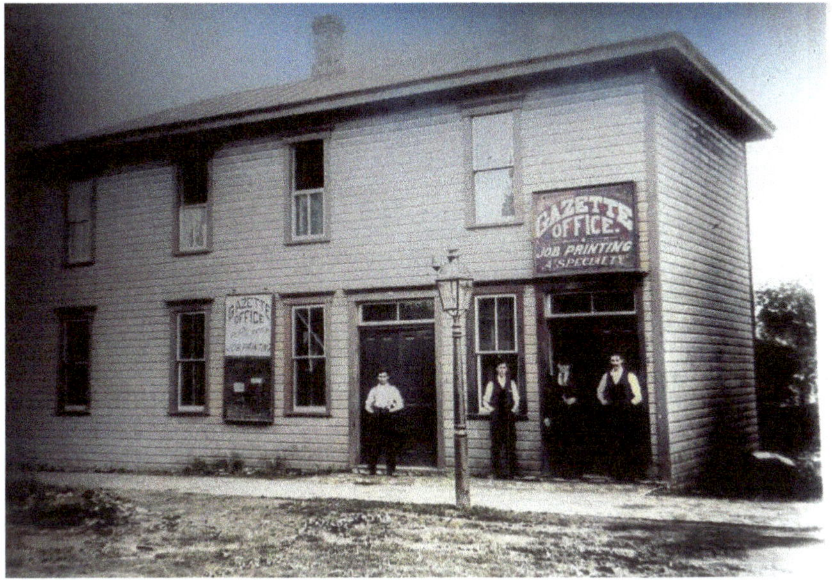

The second location of the Richwood Gazette Office located on the south side of East Ottawa Street. Photo taken circa 1880 (colorized).

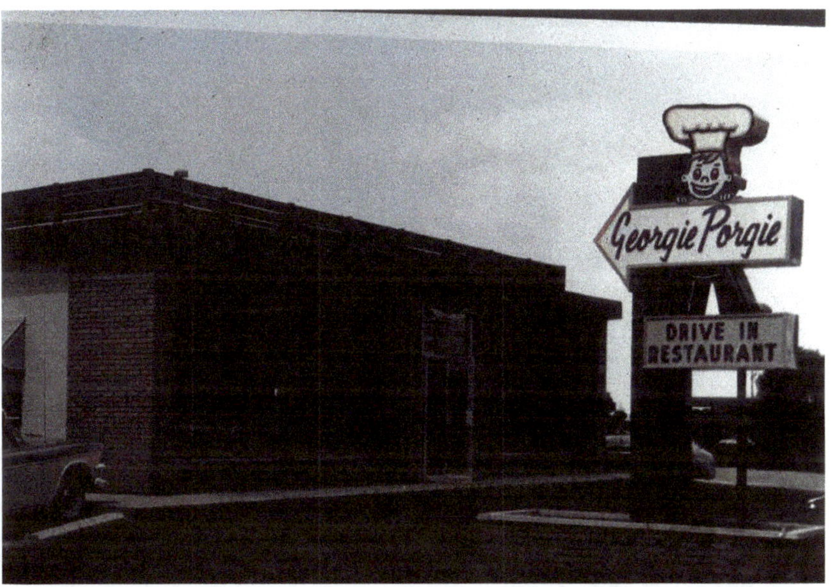

The Georgie Porgie Restaurant owned by George Keigley located on East Blagrove Street. Photo taken circa 1960 (colorized).

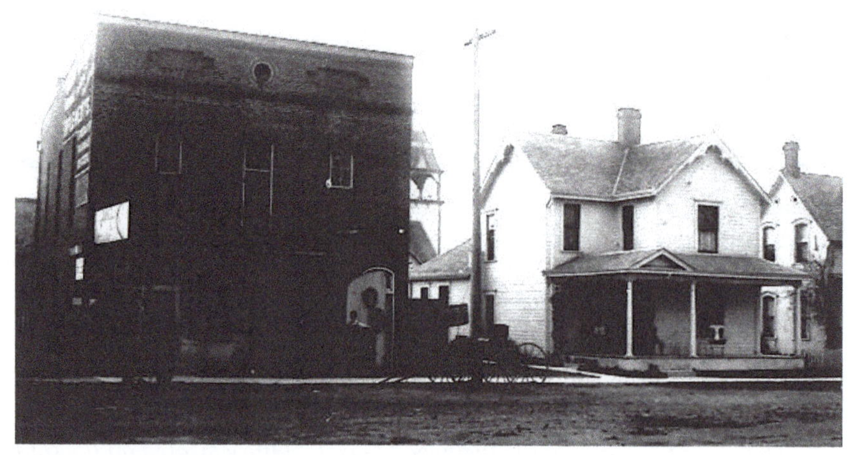

The original city building and fire (engine) house on the left. It later served as a harness shop, filling station and law office. Photo taken in 1876.

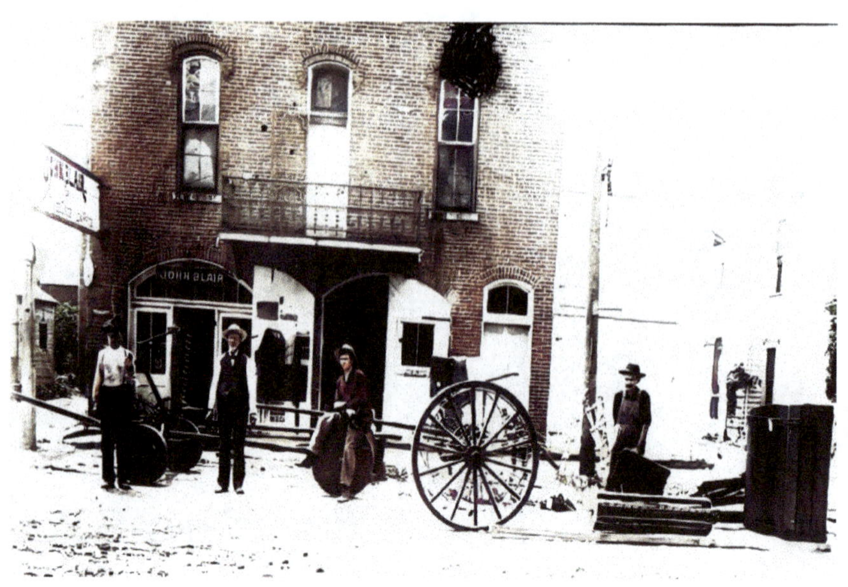

Men selling equipment at the former city building and fire house after moving to the Opera House circa 1890 (colorized).

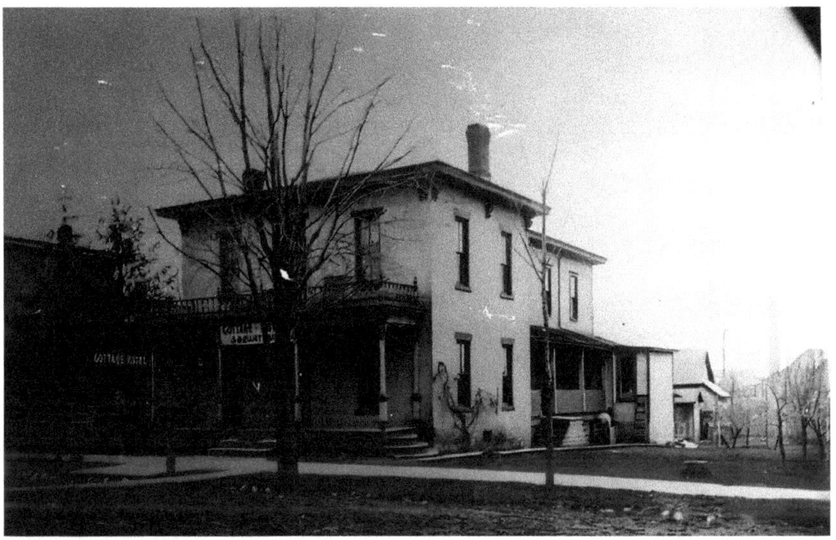

The Cottage Hotel located on North Franklin Street. The smokestack of the Beem Sawmill can be seen in the background to the right. The hotel was removed sometime in the late 1940s (colorized).

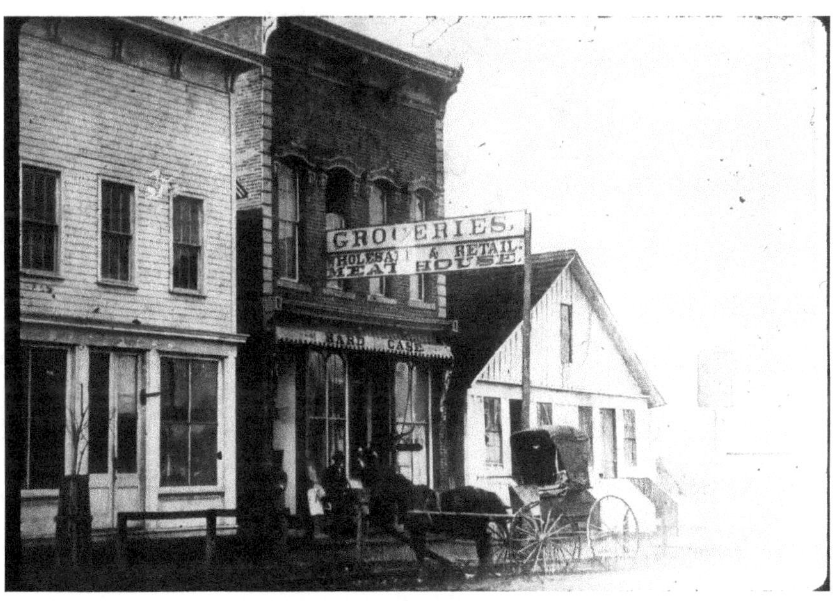

Grocery store located on Franklin Street circa 1880 (colorized).

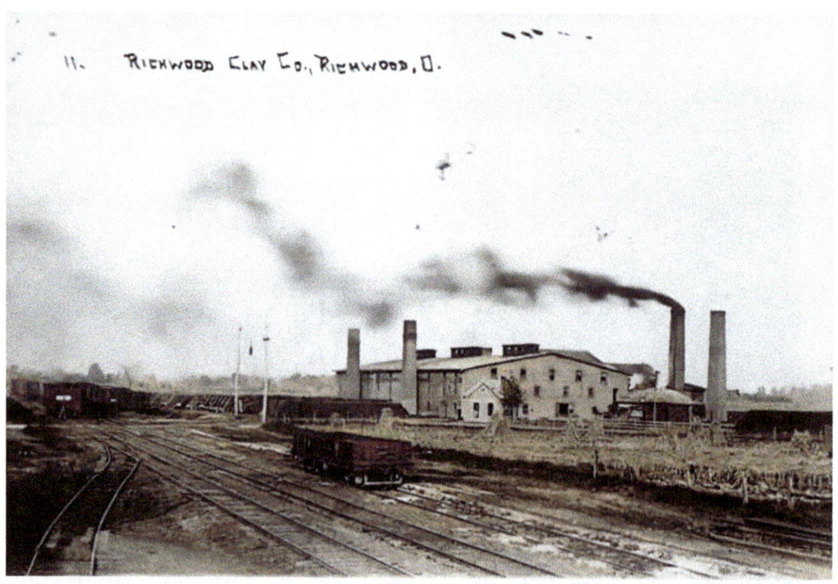

The Richwood Clay Company was located on Beatty Avenue circa 1910. It burned down in 1927 after a fire started next to a kiln on the second floor (colorized).

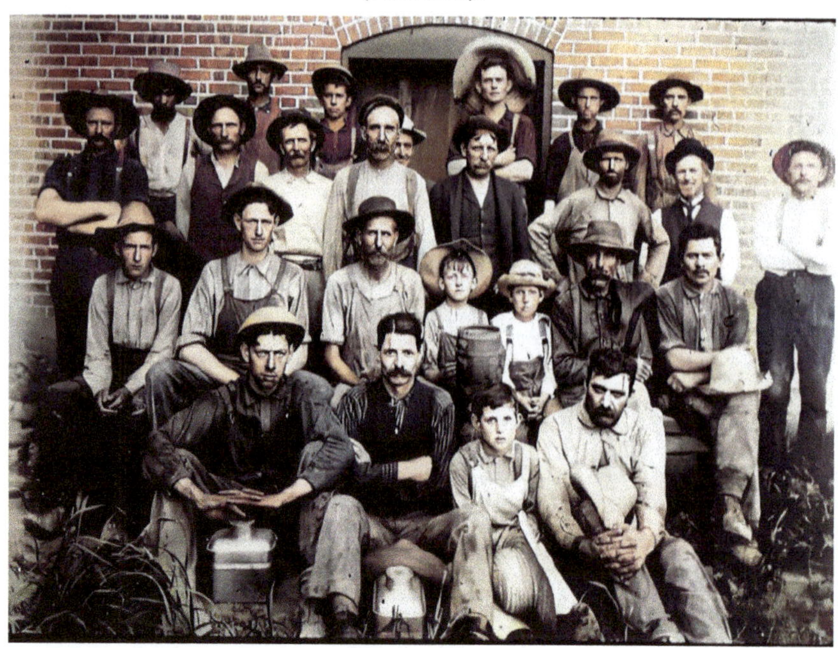

Workers at the Richwood Clay Company located on Beatty Avenue circa 1910 (colorized).

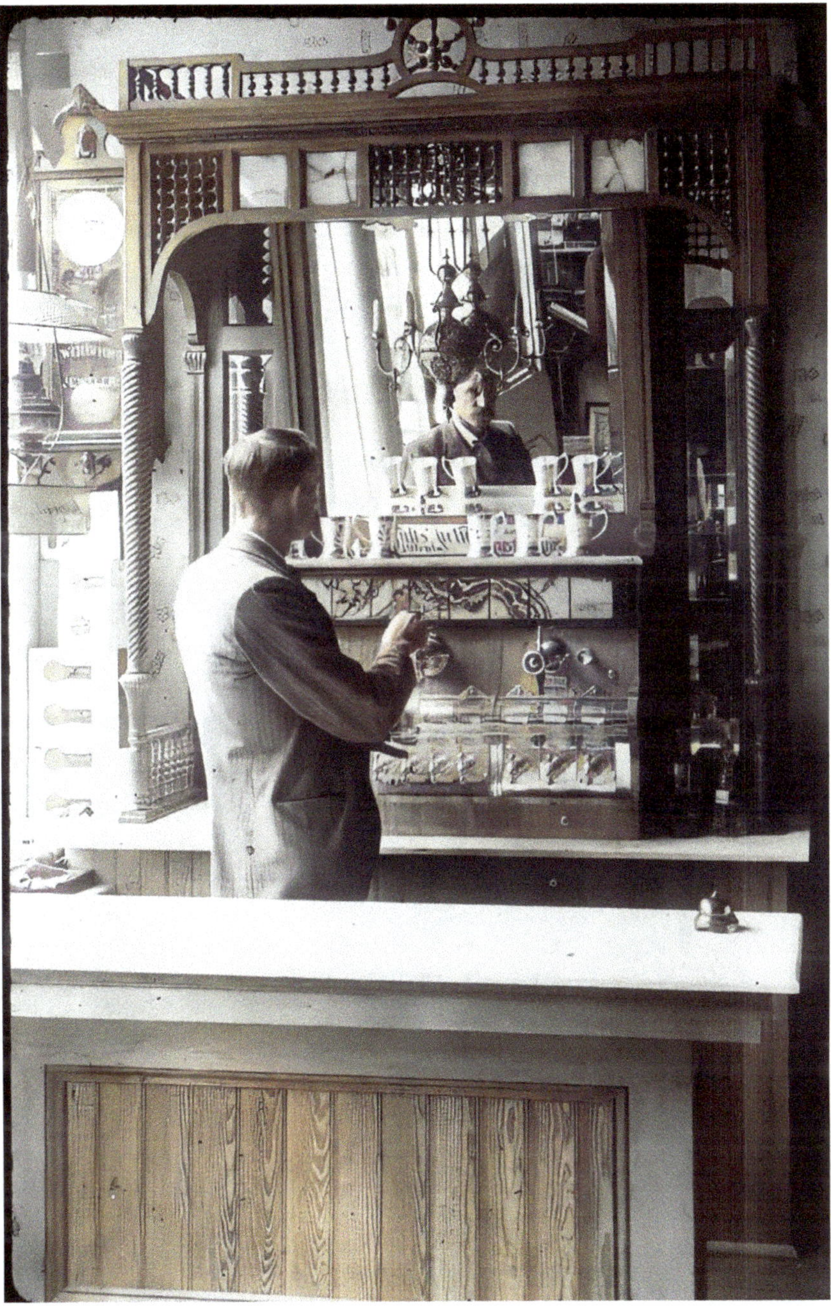

The first soda fountain in Richwood at Kyle's Drug Store circa 1920. The store was located in a three-story building that was torn down to expand the Richwood Bank which was right next door (colorized).

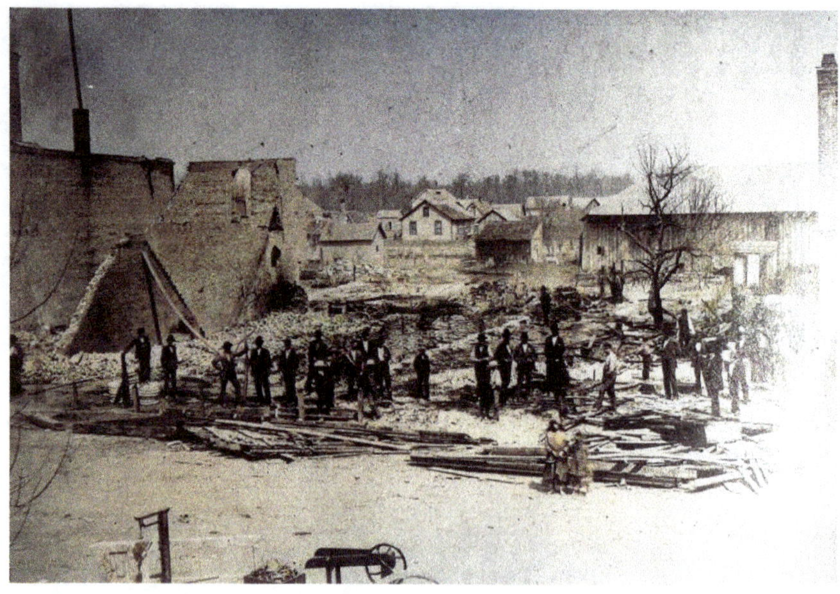

Aftermath of the fire on the east side of Franklin Street in April 1875. 8 buildings were destroyed including the Godman Thornhill Hardware Store and the Methodist Protestant Church (colorized).

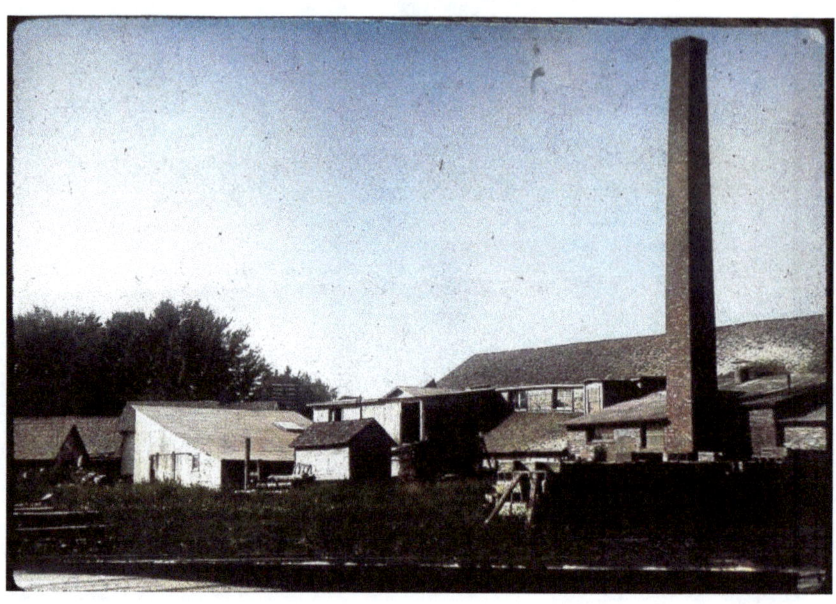

The Beem Sawmill located on the lot of the Richwood Lumber Company, which it replaced, circa 1920. It was located on what is now the baseball field at the Richwood Lake (colorized).

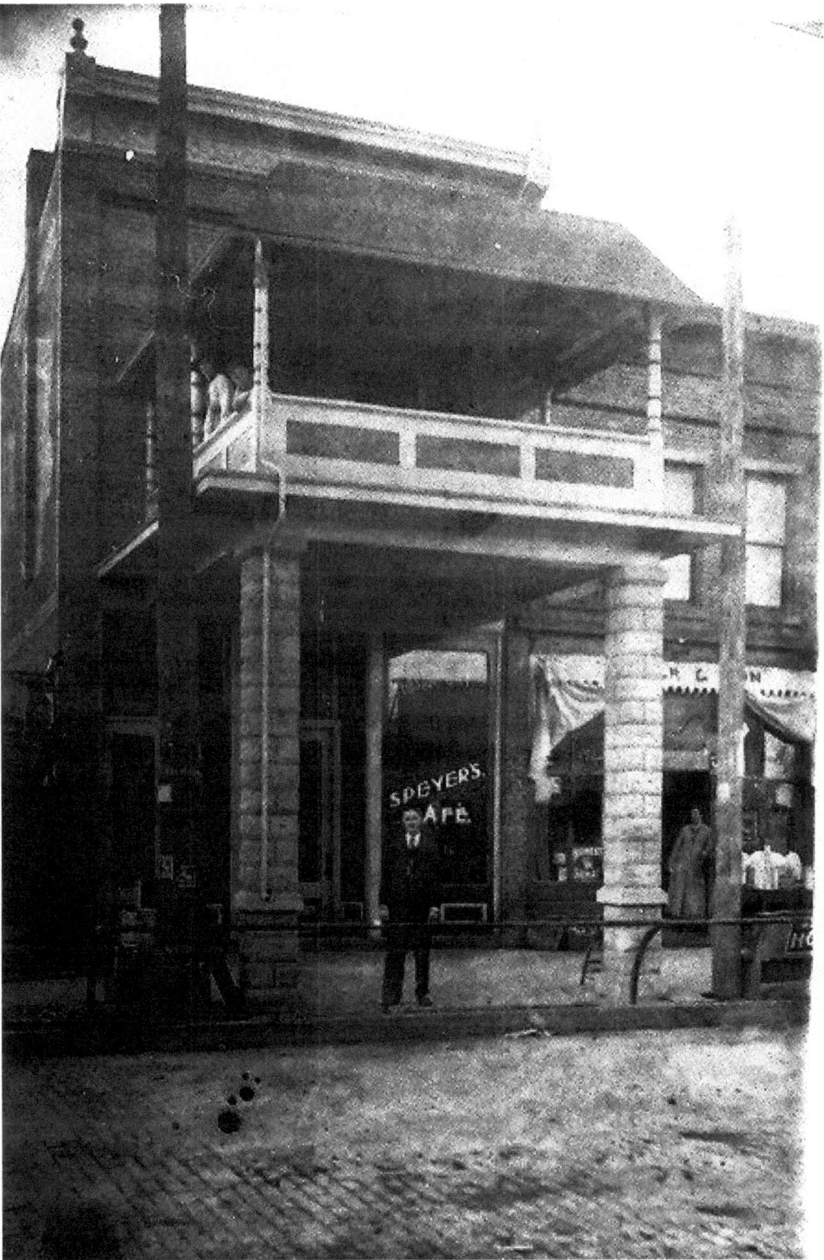

This photo is of Speyer's Café which was located to the left of what is now Toddler Scene clothing store on North Franklin Street circa 1930 (colorized).

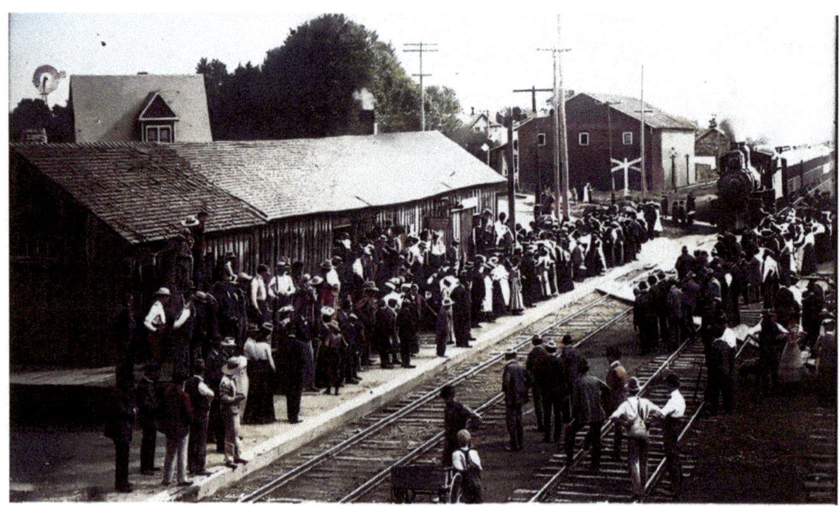

The Richwood Erie Train Depot on North Franklin Street circa 1890 (colorized).

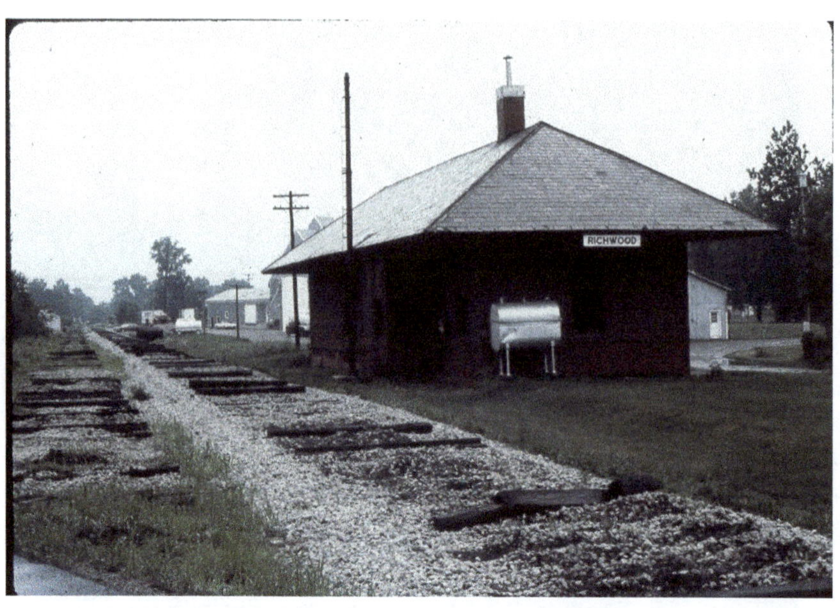

Remnants of the Richwood Erie Depot. The Erie Railroad ceased in the 1970s with the railroad track being removed around 1980. The depot is still standing, located on North Franklin Street, and is currently not in use.

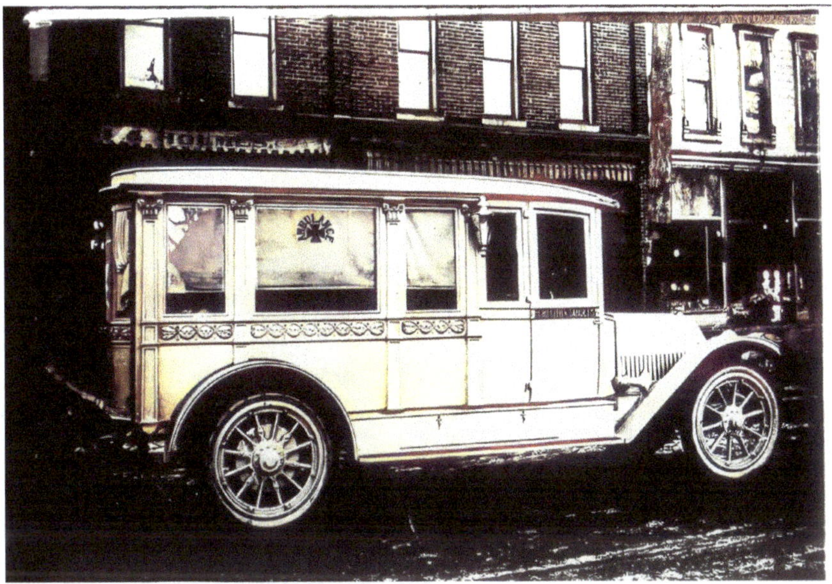

The first ambulance of Richwood owned by Sanders Funeral Home. Photo taken circa 1920 (colorized).

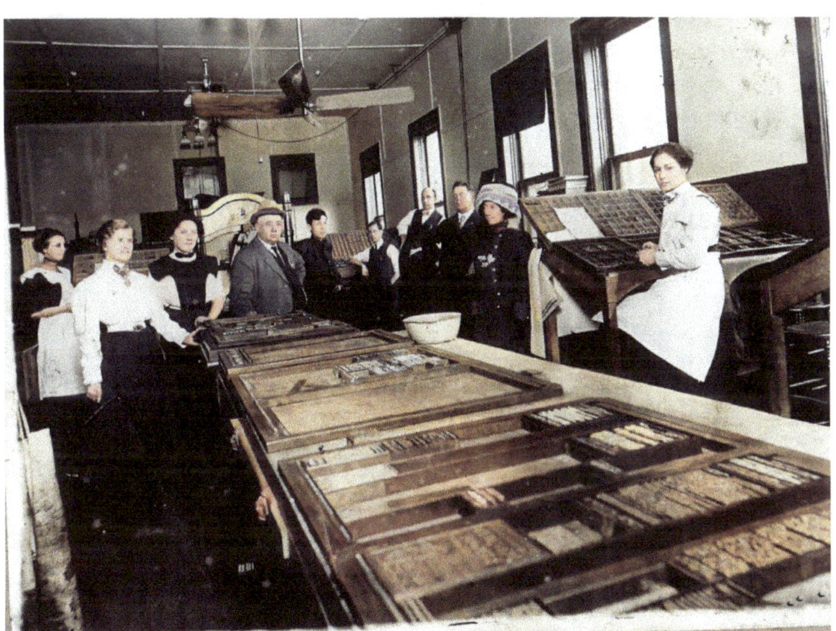

Interior of the Richwood Gazette office circa 1910. The Gazette has changed offices at least three times since its founding in 1872 (colorized).

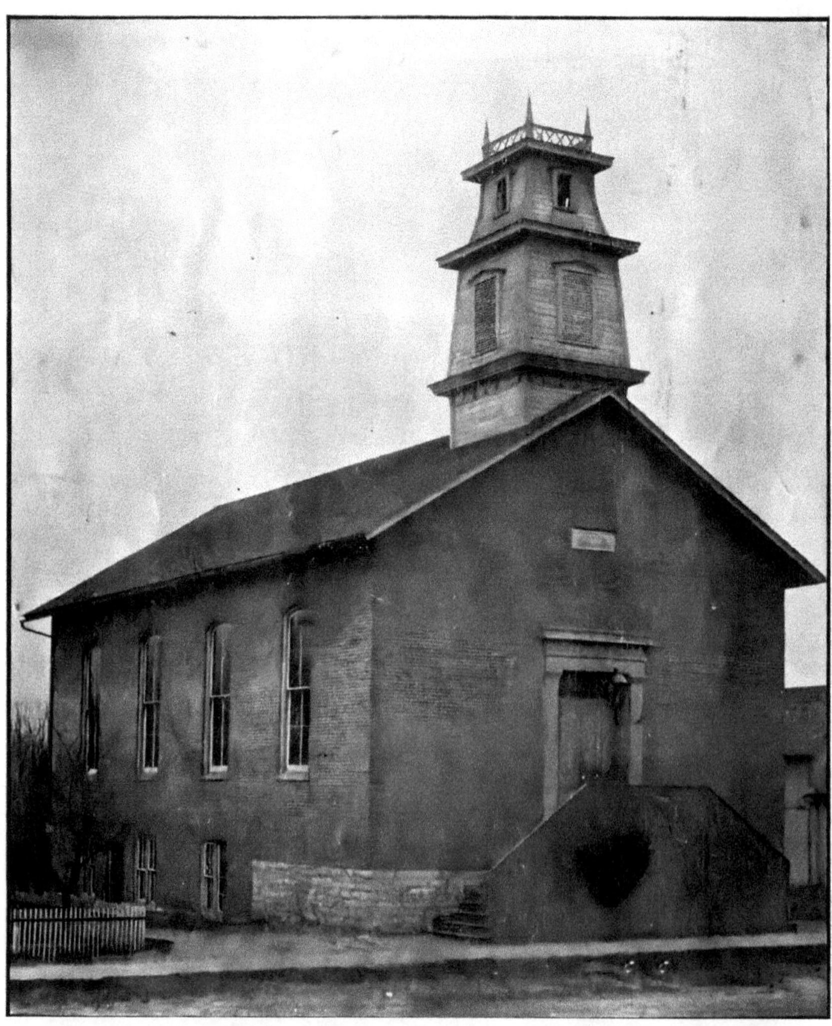

The second M.E. Church was erected in 1858, on the west side of South Fulton Street. It was torn down in 1902 after the construction of the current building which was built in 1902 in the same spot on Fulton Street where it still stands to this day (colorized).

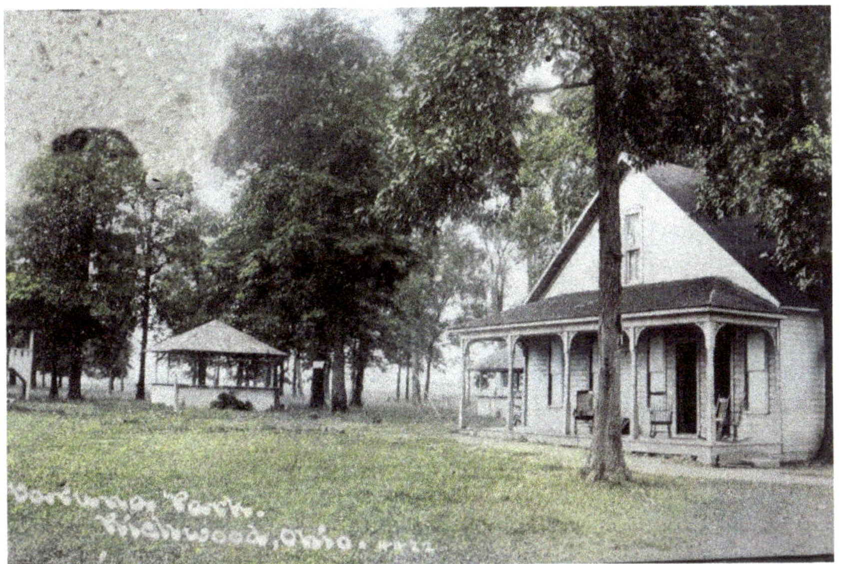

Photo of Varuna Park which was located near the fairgrounds on Race Street in 1900. The park contained a bath house, due to the discovery of mineral water in the area, along with seats, swings and a merry-go-round. A company called Varuna Water Bottling Company later started selling the mineral water until the discovery of modern medicine made mineral water, and its purported healing properties, obsolete (colorized).

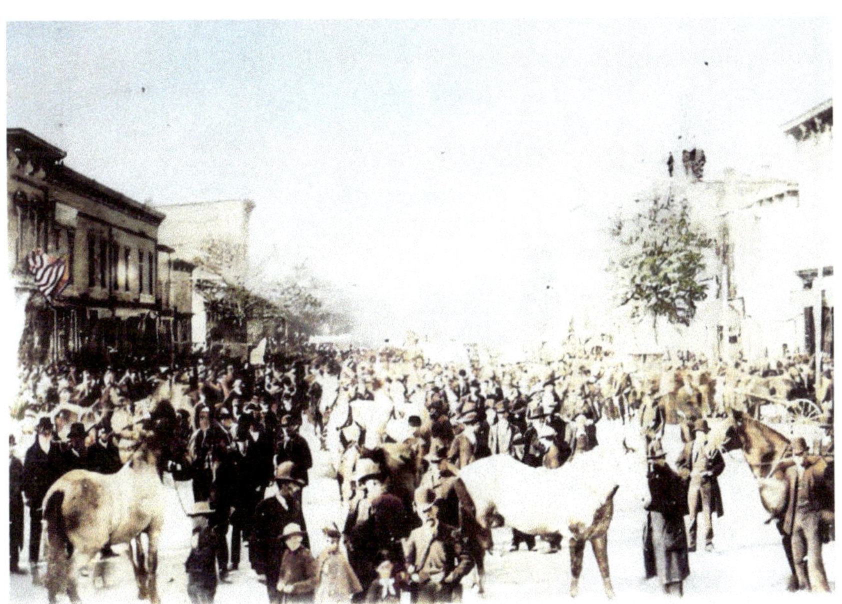

A street fair located on Franklin Street circa 1892 (colorized).

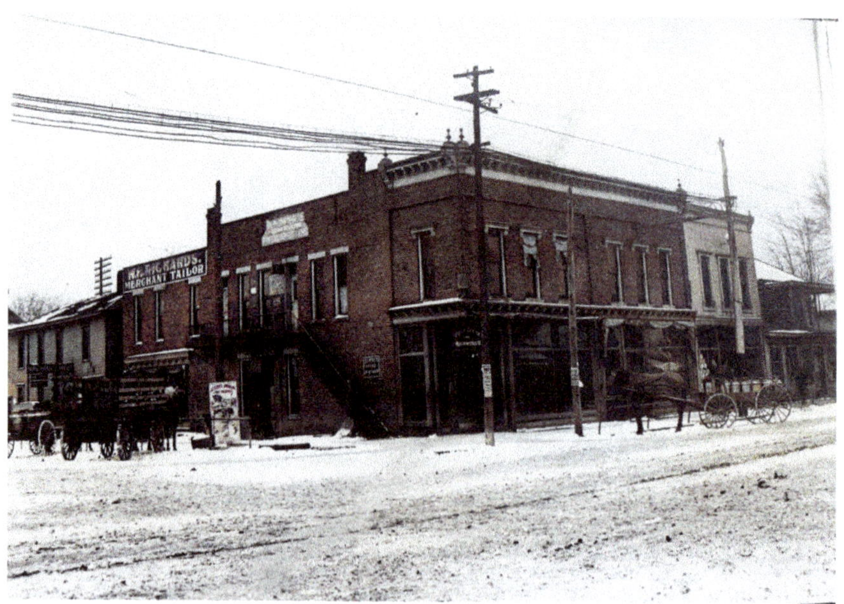

A view of the Richwood Post Office on the corner of Franklin and Ottawa Streets in 1909 (colorized).

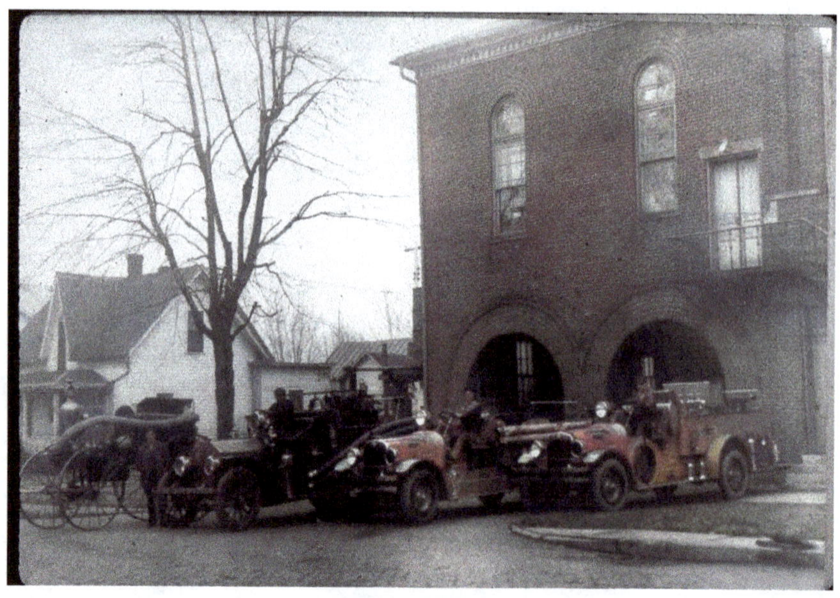

The Richwood Fire Department posing next to the Opera House circa 1930 (colorized).